RESPONDING TO THE
EVERY STUDENT SUCCEEDS ACT
WITH THE PLC AT WORK™ PROCESS

RICHARD
DuFour | DC **Reeves** | CA **DuFour**

FOREWORD BY JON SAPHIER

Solution Tree | Press

a division of
Solution Tree

555 North Morton Street
Bloomington, IN 47404
800.733.6786 (toll free) / 812.336.7700
FAX: 812.336.7790

email: info@SolutionTree.com
SolutionTree.com

Visit **go.SolutionTree.com/PLCbooks** to download the free reproducibles in this book.

Printed in the United States of America
21 20 19 18 17   1 2 3 4 5

Library of Congress Cataloging-in-Publication Data

Names: DuFour, Richard, 1947- author. | Reeves, Douglas B., 1953- author. | DuFour, Rebecca Burnette, author.
Title: Responding to the Every Student Succeeds Act with the PLC at work process / Richard DuFour, Douglas Reeves, and Rebecca DuFour.
Description: Bloomington, IN: Solution Tree Press, 2018. | Includes bibliographical references and index.
Identifiers: LCCN 2017015292 | ISBN 9781945349072 (perfect bound)
Subjects: LCSH: Educational accountability--United States. | Academic achievement--United States. | Professional learning communities--United States. | United States. Every Student Succeeds Act.
Classification: LCC LB2806.22 .D846 2018 | DDC 379.1/58--dc23 LC record available at https://lccn.loc.gov/2017015292

Solution Tree
Jeffrey C. Jones, CEO
Edmund M. Ackerman, President

Solution Tree Press
President and Publisher: Douglas M. Rife
Editorial Director: Sarah Payne-Mills
Managing Production Editor: Caroline Cascio
Senior Production Editor: Christine Hood
Senior Editor: Amy Rubenstein
Copy Editor: Evie Madsen
Proofreader: Kendra Slayton
Text and Cover Designer: Rian Anderson
Editorial Assistants: Jessi Finn and Kendra Slayton

For Rick

ACKNOWLEDGMENTS

My greatest debt is to my friends, colleagues, and coauthors—Rick and Becky DuFour—who continue to influence generations of students, teachers, and education leaders around the world.

Solution Tree Press is a collaborative enterprise that brings together ideas, authors, and readers. I am grateful for their continued support and particularly appreciate the support of Christine Hood, senior production editor; Douglas Rife, president and publisher; and Jeff Jones, chief executive officer.

—Douglas Reeves

My work on this manuscript has been very bittersweet. This is the last book that my late husband, Rick DuFour, coauthored before his death on February 8, 2017. I have vivid memories of our collaboration with one another and with our wonderful friend and coauthor, Doug Reeves, on this important project in the final months of Rick's life. Rick was so hopeful that this book would guide educators and policymakers at all levels to understand the opportunities the Every Student Succeeds Act offers and to embrace our collective responsibility to ensure that every student truly will be successful in school and set for success in life. I, too, am hopeful and proud to be a torchbearer of the PLC at Work™ process, a powerful continuous improvement process that ensures learning for all U.S. children and the adults who serve them.

Rick and I owe a tremendous debt of gratitude to Jeff Jones, the CEO of Solution Tree, and to the entire Solution Tree and Solution Tree Press families. Solution Tree has supported, advanced, and published our work for almost twenty years. Although most of the Solution Tree staff members are not professional educators, they work tirelessly to provide the ongoing professional learning that must occur as educators strive to help all students learn at high levels. Please visit www.SolutionTree.com/about/overview to learn more about Solution Tree and its vision of transforming education worldwide.

Like Rick was, I will be forever grateful for the amazing team of PLC at Work associates—currently about 140 members strong—that Solution Tree continues to grow and support. I learn so much from these dedicated practitioners who have led the PLC process in their own settings and are willing and able to share their time and expertise with other educators, often at the expense of time with their own families. Please visit www.SolutionTree.com/presenters/l/professional-learning-communities-at-work-trade.html to meet the members of this amazing team of professional educators.

Finally, I want to acknowledge and honor the educators who devote their life's work—their time, energy, passion, and expertise—to making a positive difference in the lives of every student entrusted to them. Your work is difficult, demanding, and so very important. To quote my all-time favorite author and teacher, Rick DuFour, as he ended every keynote presentation in the last few years: "I believe in you. Godspeed."

—Becky DuFour

Solution Tree Press would like to thank the following reviewers:

Kevin Fitzgerald
Superintendent
Caesar Rodney School District
Wyoming, Delaware

Blane McCann
Superintendent
Westside Community Schools
Omaha, Nebraska

Eddie Ingram
Superintendent
Darlington County School
    District
Darlington, South Carolina

Susan Rieke-Smith
Superintendent
Springfield Public Schools
Springfield, Oregon

Amanda Lemanczyk Ross
Associate Superintendent
Ames Community School
  District
Ames, Iowa

Rhonda Schmidt
Elementary PD and Curriculum
  Facilitator
West Des Moines Community
  Schools
West Des Moines, Iowa

Mike Stiemsma
School Improvement Consultant
Great Prairie Area Education
  Agency
Fairfield, Iowa

Visit **go.SolutionTree.com/PLCbooks** to download the free reproducibles in this book.

TABLE OF CONTENTS

APPENDIX A
Sample School-Level Accountability Indicators . . . 117

APPENDIX B
Sample System-Level Accountability Indicators . . . 129

References and Resources

Index

ABOUT THE AUTHORS

 **Richard DuFour, EdD,** was a public school educator for thirty-four years, serving as a teacher, principal, and superintendent. During his nineteen-year tenure as both principal and superintendent at Adlai E. Stevenson High School in Lincolnshire, Illinois, Stevenson became one of only three schools in the nation to win the U.S. Department of Education Blue Ribbon Award on four occasions and the first comprehensive high school to be designated a New America High School as a model of successful school reform. Rick received his state's highest award as both a principal and superintendent.

A prolific author and sought-after consultant, Rick was recognized as one of the leading authorities on helping school practitioners implement the Professional Learning Communities at Work™ process in their schools and districts.

Rick wrote a quarterly column for the *Journal of Staff Development* for nearly a decade. He was the lead consultant and author of the Association for Supervision and Curriculum Development's video series on principalship and the author of several other videos. Rick was named as one of the Top 100 School Administrators in North America by *Executive Educator* magazine, was presented the Distinguished Scholar Practitioner Award from the University of Illinois, and was the 2004 recipient of the National Staff Development Council's Distinguished Service Award.

To learn more about Rick's work, visit AllThingsPLC (www.all thingsplc.info).

Douglas Reeves, PhD, is the author of more than thirty books and many articles about leadership and organizational effectiveness. He was named the Brock International Laureate for his contributions to education and received the Contribution to the Field Award from the National Staff Development Council (now Learning Forward). Douglas has addressed audiences in all fifty U.S. states and more than twenty-five countries, sharing his research and supporting effective leadership at the local, state, and national levels. He is founder of Finish the Dissertation, a free and noncommercial service for doctoral students, and the Zambian Leadership and Learning Institute. He is the founding editor and copublisher of *The SNAFU Review*, a collection of essays, poetry, and art by veterans suffering from post-traumatic stress disorder. Douglas lives with his family in downtown Boston.

To learn more about Douglas's work, visit Creative Leadership Solutions (https://creativeleadership.net) or the *Change Leaders* blog (www.changeleaders.com), or follow @DouglasReeves on Twitter.

Rebecca DuFour, M.Ed., has served as a teacher, school administrator, and central office coordinator. As a former elementary principal, she helped her school earn state and national recognition as a model professional learning community and as a National Blue Ribbon School. She is coauthor of twelve books, numerous articles, and several video resources on the topic of PLCs.

Serving as a consultant for more than sixteen years, Becky brings more than thirty-five years of professional experience to her work with educators around the world who are implementing the PLC process in their own organizations. Becky is the recipient of the Distinguished Alumni Award of Lynchburg College. She consults with professional organizations, schools, districts, universities, and departments of education.

To learn more about Becky's work, visit AllThingsPLC (www.all thingsplc.info).

To book Douglas Reeves or Rebecca DuFour for professional development, contact pd@SolutionTree.com.

▌ FOREWORD ▌

by Jon Saphier

Communicating with utmost clarity and doing so about highly important policies is a rare combination, but it has always been a hallmark of Rick and Becky DuFour's presentations, whether in person or in writing. In this book, Doug Reeves joins them in making a case that cries out for the attention of policymakers.

All three write with a sense of urgency, provoked by the abundance of knowledge we now have about how to use data to improve student learning and the perilous slide in the opposite direction U.S. national and state policies have induced. The PLC movement has given us the tools to study student results and turn that information into energetic reteaching and accelerated learning for those who are discouraged and those who are behind. Instead, measurement and accountability have been used as cleavers to sort and rank teachers rather than tools to analyze and improve student learning.

Teaching expertise includes skills for frequently gathering student-learning data, skillfully analyzing the data, and inventively and encouragingly reteaching content to those who didn't get it the first time around. The PLC movement has always been about the promise and the skillful practice of these arts. Far beyond stand-up presenting, skillful teaching includes anything a person does that increases the probability of intended learning.

The belief that ability can be grown and "smart is something you can get" (Howard, 1995, page 90) has always been embedded in the DuFours' work. That belief emerges prominently in this book. Call it growth mindset or effort-based ability; that belief provides the drive and commitment to make PLCs really work. We simply cannot allow ourselves to leave any child behind. And we can actually ensure that comes true!

The difficult work of solving complex learning problems requires teamwork and multiple minds. A solo practitioner in medicine, law, or engineering is bound to fail often. That is why they do not work alone but with deep consultation and collaboration in teams.

Deep collaboration in any field means learning how to function skillfully and nondefensively with others in teams. In education, these teams are composed of individuals who teach the same content. They use data about student performance to improve teaching and learning. Regrettably, such skill is rarely part of teacher education, but it is a vital part of professional expertise. It is up to our whole profession to make sure this skill is developed over one's career path and to lawmakers and policymakers to ensure resources and accountability are in place to make that happen.

What the authors have laid out for us in this volume is the marriage of two skill sets that are missing in action from educators' career development. One is analytical (the study of student data leading to error analysis and reteaching), and the other is interpersonal (how to communicate effectively and interact nondefensively in the interest of students' learning).

Certain schools may get by without teachers who know how to use the full range of extant knowledge about and skill with PLCs and about teaching and learning if their students come from high-expectations families and affluence. These students may have the experience of having been read to since the age of two, or the experience of travel, museums, music lessons, sports teams with coaching, lively dinner conversations, family picnics, national parks, or camping. But highly developed collaborative practice is required for many of our children of poverty, and if we could generate enough of it, we wouldn't have the intractable achievement gap we do today. That is a fact documented every single year by schools highlighted on the Education Trust's website.

The achievement gap for children of color and of poverty is one with devastating consequences for our youngsters, our workforce, and our economy, but most of all our democracy. We used to be the land of opportunity, and our institutions (churches, clubs, and community organizations) supported that narrative. We are becoming the land of inequality with permanent residency for those trapped by poor education.

The promise of democracy is a fair chance at a good life. This book includes the prescriptions for how our education system can be the promise keeper. There's plenty of practical advice for practitioners at all levels, like interview questions that uncover teachers' beliefs about learning, about responsibility, and about students' capacity to learn. But at bottom, this book is a compelling case for "ongoing, job-embedded learning of the adults" (page 2), about expertise, and about powerful use of data with deeply collaborative analysis. Policymakers take note: ongoing learning is the "key to improved learning for students" (page 2). Everything needs to be organized around that.

INTRODUCTION

A question relevant to readers and writers alike is: "Who is the intended audience for this work?" A potential reader may frame the question a slightly different way: "Am I included in the intended audience?" or "Will reading this benefit me in some way?" A writer will ask: "Who am I attempting to influence?"

When a book is intended to appeal to a wide range of stakeholders, the challenge of answering the "Who am I attempting to influence?" question becomes considerably more daunting. In this introduction, we hope to clarify our intention to focus on the wider audience—both legislative and educational. We'll examine the Every Student Succeeds Act (ESSA, 2015) and explain why it must address the interests of a wider range of stakeholders rather than those of a particular interest group. This broader approach operates on the assumption that people in different parts of an organization can find common ground if they make it a priority to do so.

The Professional Learning Communities at Work™ (PLC) process has helped hundreds of schools and entire districts go from underperforming to high achieving, from good to great, and from great to greater (DuFour, DuFour, Eaker, Many, & Mattos, 2016). (Visit www .allthingsplc.info/evidence to see numerous models of the PLC at Work process around the world.)

PLC schools and districts implement processes that drive continuous improvement throughout the organization. The educators within the organization recognize that the key to improved learning for students is the ongoing, job-embedded learning of the adults who serve those students. Therefore, educators in a PLC no longer work in isolation ("my classroom," "my students") but rather work in collaborative teams. Collaborative team members take collective responsibility for ensuring that each student in their course, discipline, or grade learns at high levels—grade level or better—each year.

A PLC school's master schedule is aligned to the number-one priority of the school: ensuring high levels of learning for all. Educators learn with and from each other because time is allocated each week for teams to work and learn together. Collaborative team members within a PLC school or district work collaboratively to:

- Agree on the most important skills, concepts, and dispositions every student must learn

- Monitor each student's learning on a frequent basis using team-developed common assessments

- Analyze student-learning results to determine which students are struggling to learn and which students have demonstrated proficiency

- Share instructional practices with one another that proved to be effective, based on the student-learning results from their common assessments

- Use their joint analysis of evidence of student learning to set goals for continuous improvement

The school, rather than the individual classroom teacher, guarantees students receive extra time and support to learn beyond daily classroom instruction during a period of the school day specifically designated for extra support. When students struggle to learn, based on the results of team common assessments, the support is timely and targeted intervention. When students have demonstrated high levels of learning, the extra support is designed to extend their learning.

When the PLC process is implemented unit by unit in each course and grade level, students and educators continually learn at higher levels. The success of each student is impacted not by one teacher to whom the student has been assigned but rather by a caring and skillful team of teachers who take collective responsibility for the learning of each student and each other.

A Rare Opportunity

Americans interested in public education in the United States have a rare opportunity. The passage of ESSA gives stakeholders in education the chance to redefine the purpose, priorities, and processes of schooling.

The key word in the preceding paragraph is *opportunity*, rather than *certainty*. In this book, we will demonstrate the following.

> *The passage of ESSA gives stakeholders in education the chance to redefine the purpose, priorities, and processes of schooling.*

- The passage of ESSA represents a significant policy change from prior legislation and regulations.

- The authority of the U.S. Secretary of Education has been drastically diminished by the passage of ESSA. In fact, the legislation prohibits the secretary from making recommendations dealing with curriculum and instruction.

- States now have the ability to establish their own new and unique goals, standards, curriculum, evaluation processes, incentives, and punishments.

- One of the challenges at the state level is to determine whether state departments of education will use their increased authority to identify creative ways to improve schools and help more students learn at high levels, or whether they will continue to pursue the ill-advised, failed policies from 2001 through 2016: the No Child Left Behind (NCLB) Act, enacted in 2001 and signed by President George W. Bush, and supported by majorities in both parties; and the Race to the Top (RTTT) initiative established by President Barack Obama in 2009.

- Another challenge at the state level is communicating with more than fourteen thousand U.S. school districts (United

States Census Bureau, n.d.) in a way that provides clarity of purpose and a shared common vision of schooling.

- At the local level, educators must come to a common understanding of how ESSA can impact their day-to-day work. Ultimately, we will call on them to build their collective capacity to embrace the following two key ideas.

  a. All students can learn.

  b. The entire staff shares a collective responsibility to support the academic success of every student.

- The most promising strategy for sustained and substantive school improvement is developing the capacity of the staff to function as members of high-performing teams in schools that are true professional learning communities.

- Local education leaders must explain changes in policy to parents and other stakeholders. Without such clear and consistent communication, parents can easily default to their own experience—the way school was when they were students.

The Audience

So, who is the audience for this book? In a perfect world, every state legislature would become deeply familiar with this book's contents. Lawmakers would be persuaded to move away from the punitive-based, sanction-driven reforms of the past and use this book to help clarify how states can improve student learning by embracing PLC principles. We will address the specifics of those principles. However, this is more than a manual for policymakers. The practical advice in the following pages will be useful for leaders at the district, school, and classroom levels.

During the first decade and a half of the 21st century, education leaders asked, "What does Washington want?" as they attempted to avoid the sanctions of No Child Left Behind and pursue the incentives of Race to the Top. But with the advent of ESSA, education leaders must ask, "What do the students in my system need?" The implementation of the PLC process and the other ideas in this book is not merely a response to national legislation but rather an ethical imperative. These are the right things to do and not an exercise in compliance with higher authorities.

But ultimately, the impact of ESSA on student learning in the United States depends on the quality of educators students meet with each day. *Collective efficacy*—the belief that our combined efforts can have a positive impact in achieving our shared goals—is one of the strongest predictors of an improving school. The PLC process, when implemented well, is our best strategy for increasing teacher, administrator, and student efficacy.

> *But ultimately, the impact of ESSA on student learning in the United States depends on the quality of educators students meet with each day.*

Out of Chaos Comes Order

To outside observers, the U.S. education system reflects chaos. It involves 14,000 independent school districts, 150,000 schools, and more than 48 million students—with no national agreement on what students should know at any given grade level, no comprehensive exam that assesses everything students should learn, and no consensus on what schools should do when students struggle to learn (United States Census Bureau, n.d.).

If the U.S. education system is ever to operate as a true *system*, it must embrace clarity of purpose, a guaranteed and viable curriculum, careful monitoring of each student's learning, and a prompt intervention process that ensures the staff continues to provide struggling students extra time and support until they become proficient.

Educators and legislators who work together to create a true system of education in their districts and schools can offer action research to help others learn from their work. In short, the years to come can be the best of times for schooling in the United States *if our legislatures and districts fully commit to the PLC process.* But if lawmakers and educators cling to the failed

> *In short, the years to come can be the best of times for schooling in the United States if our legislatures and districts fully commit to the PLC process.*

policies of the past—policies that view teachers as problems to solve rather than resources to develop—ESSA will have little impact on student achievement.

In the Face of Uncertainty

Political uncertainty in every era pushes education leaders into one of two directions. The first, and most common, is the path of *paralysis*: "We can't respond until we know what to do," these leaders lament. This strikes us as curious, as the same leaders often express deep resentment of policy hierarchies that have, during the years 2001–2016, issued one directive after another. Most of these policy prescriptions, particularly those associated with accountability systems based on student test scores and Byzantine teacher evaluation systems (no offense intended to the Byzantine Empire), have been counterproductive. Time that could have been profitably devoted to teaching and learning has been diverted to test prep and mind-numbing documentation of teacher evaluation systems.

But now that schools, districts, and states have been liberated from these restrictions, education leaders following the first path remain paralyzed, waiting for one bureaucratic system to be replaced by another, as if toxic micromanagement from a national capital would magically be better displaced by the same policies from a state capital.

There is a better way, and that is the path this book suggests. Schools, districts, and states can pursue a new way—*accountability as a learning system*. They can focus on known best practices in teaching and learning, with collaborative work among teachers and administrators at every level. We believe that the fundamental purpose of educational accountability is improving student learning through improved teaching and leadership practices. This is in stark contrast to those who believe that the purpose of educational accountability is to rate, rank, evaluate, and humiliate schools and the teachers and administrators who work there.

While we know that schools should not be immune from criticism, we have seen no evidence that criticism, ratings, and rankings have led to improved student achievement. At the heart of the PLC process is a continuous source of feedback that helps students, teachers, and administrators understand how to improve. Just as PLCs are a *learning system* for collaborative teams of teachers, our vision of accountability is that the PLC framework can help entire districts, states, and ultimately the world.

We write with a sense of urgency. As the following chapters demonstrate, education systems have an unprecedented opportunity to redefine in fundamental terms what the phrase *educational accountability* really means. Readers will discover the opportunity to engage in fundamental transformation, from accountability as a means for public humiliation, supported by dubious and opaque statistical systems, to accountability as a learning system, one that helps students, teachers, education leaders, and policymakers use the information from accountability systems to inform professional practice and policymaking in real time.

> *Education systems have an unprecedented opportunity to redefine in fundamental terms what the phrase* educational accountability *really means.*

After considering the history of education oversight in the United States in chapter 1, we then examine ESSA and how states can respond to this legislation in chapters 2 and 3. In chapter 4, we provide an example of how an individual school might respond to ESSA, elevating collaboration over a tradition of competitive private practice. In chapters 5 and 6, we consider how districts and states, respectively, can respond to ESSA. In these chapters, we offer a three-tiered accountability system in which districts and states consider accountability indicators that are common to all schools, such as safety and academic achievement, and illuminate these results with accountability indicators that are unique to the needs of each individual school. Our theme in these chapters is that accountability is more than a litany of test scores. Educational accountability becomes a learning system only when effects—student achievement—are linked to causes—specific actions of teachers, leaders, parents, and policymakers. Finally, in chapter 7, we consider the path ahead for ESSA.

Let us state at the outset that this is not the time for education leaders to wait and see what might happen in terms of state and federal policymaking. Rather, we ask these provocative questions: "Under what conceivable political or economic environment will effective teaching and leadership *not* be important? Under what set of circumstances will the best professional practices available (teacher collaboration through the PLC at Work process) *not* be the most effective and professional path for teachers and leaders to follow? What level of uncertainty would justify decision-making paralysis by teachers, administrators, and policymakers?"

In sum, we ask you to consider the evidence and practices in the following pages not because they are a reflection of legislation and regulations but rather because responding to ESSA through the PLC at Work process is the right thing to do under any law, administration, or political environment. The time for action is *now*. There is no excuse for delay. There is no justification for temporizing. Our students and our communities deserve our best, and they deserve it immediately.

CHAPTER 1

A Brief History of Education Oversight in the United States

n December 2015, Americans witnessed an event even rarer than a lunar eclipse. A deeply divided and fractious U.S. Congress passed a significant piece of legislation with strong bipartisan support. That law, the Every Student Succeeds Act (ESSA, 2015), is the latest reauthorization of the Elementary and Secondary Education Act originally passed in 1965. ESSA redefines the role of the federal government in K–12 education and, in many ways, is a dramatic departure from the previous No Child Left Behind Act (NCLB, 2002) and the Race to the Top program (U.S. Department of Education, 2009). The authority of states and districts to oversee their own school-improvement processes is significantly enhanced, while the role of the federal government in school reform and accountability is dramatically reduced. Before examining the details and potential of the new law, let's briefly review past U.S. education-reform efforts and how the federal government contributed to those efforts.

A Look Back

According to the Tenth Amendment of the U.S. Constitution, "The powers not delegated to the United States by the Constitution, nor prohibited by it to the States, are reserved to the States respectively, or to the people" (U.S. Const. amend. X). This provision provides the basis of the legal theory that education is a function of the states rather than the federal government. The U.S. Supreme Court and the state courts have consistently ruled that education is one of the powers reserved for the states.

However, Brown v. Board of Education (1954) established that the federal government could limit the authority of the states when it comes to education. The plaintiffs in the case argued that state-sanctioned racially segregated schools should be ruled unconstitutional because they violate the Fourteenth Amendment's provision that citizens cannot be denied equal protection of the law (U.S. Const. amend. XIV). The defendants argued that the issue had been repeatedly addressed in the courts from the time of Plessy v. Ferguson (1896), which authorized "separate but equal" schools, and the courts consistently supported racial segregation if the state provided equal facilities to both races.

John Davis, a renowned attorney representing the defendants, argued before the court, "This court has not once but seven times, I think, pronounced in favor of the 'separate but equal' doctrine" (as cited in Blaustein & Zangrando, 1991, p. 430).

Davis also pressed the doctrine of states' rights under Article X, arguing:

> Neither this Court nor any other court, I respectfully submit, can sit in the chairs of the legislature of South Carolina and mold its educational map. . . . It establishes the schools, it pays the funds, and it has the sole power to educate its citizens. (as cited in Friedman, 2003)

The Supreme Court rejected that argument in a unanimous decision, ruling that racially segregated schools were "inherently unequal" and should be integrated "with all deliberate speed" (Friedman, 2003). This ruling established that, under the right circumstances, the federal government could indeed play a role in K–12 education.

Federal Inroads Into K–12 Education

In 1965, the administration of President Lyndon Johnson used Article I, Section 8 of the Constitution to persuade the U.S. Congress to further strengthen the federal role in education. That section of the Constitution specifically gave Congress authority to "lay and collect taxes . . . to pay the Debts and provide for the common defense and general welfare of the United States" (U.S. Const., art. I, § 8). Citing this "general welfare" clause, Congress passed the Elementary and Secondary Education Act of 1965 (ESEA) to provide "financial assistance . . . to local educational agencies serving areas with concentrations of children from low-income families to expand and improve their educational programs" (Social Welfare History Project, n.d.).

President Johnson described the legislation as "the most sweeping educational bill ever to come before Congress. . . . As President of the United States, I believe deeply no law I have signed or will ever sign means more to the future of America" (Franklin, Harris, & Allen-Meares, 2006, p. 873).

The law was careful, however, not to totally circumvent the states. Each state could apply for ESEA block grants, and money would flow through the states to the local district. Furthermore, the 1965 legislation stipulated that no funds could be used to create a national curriculum. Matters regarding what students should learn and how their learning should be monitored continued to be reserved to the states. Nevertheless, this law provided the principal means through which the federal government provided funds to schools, communities, and children for education purposes. As Kris Sloan (2007) concludes:

> Forty years of sustained federal commitment under the ESEA has changed the face of public education in the United States in many ways. Title I has helped bolster the academic achievement of millions of disadvantaged children particularly in mathematics and literacy. . . . The Title II Eisenhower Professional Development program has exposed thousands of classroom teachers to new professional knowledge and instructional techniques in mathematics, science, and other critical subject areas. Title VII, Bilingual Education, has helped generations of immigrant children learn English and succeed in school. These and other ESEA-sponsored programs have benefited numerous students, teachers, and parents. (p. 16)

Although ESEA was originally authorized for five years, Congress reauthorized and modified the law ten times between 1965 and 2015.

Although ESEA was originally authorized for five years, Congress reauthorized and modified the law ten times between 1965 and 2015. Both the NCLB Act of 2002 and the ESSA of 2015 are reauthorizations of this initial legislative effort to provide the federal government with a greater voice in K–12 public education. During these years, the call for school reform was never-ending—and the call came from many different sources.

Never-Ending School Reform

In 1983, President Ronald Reagan's National Commission on Excellence in Education presented its conclusions regarding the quality of schooling in the United States in a hyperbolic report titled *A Nation at Risk*. The commission asserted that U.S. education had fallen victim to a "rising tide of mediocrity that threatens our very future as a nation and a people" (National Commission on Excellence in Education, 1983). The report was complete with dire warnings of decline, deficiencies, threats, risks, afflictions, and plight. Americans were urged to reverse the "unthinking, unilateral educational disarmament" that had taken hold of our schools and reestablish the United States as the world leader in educational attainment (National Commission on Excellence in Education, n.d.). To address the crisis, the commission called for *more*—more hours in the school day, more days in the school year, more standardized tests, more credits required for graduation, and more homework. Soon thereafter, more than three hundred different organizations issued proposals for reforming our schools.

In 1989, President George H. W. Bush attempted to gently interject a federal voice into the education reform discussion when he convened U.S. governors for a summit on education to establish national goals for education. To achieve the ambitious goals established at the summit (including that U.S. students would rank first in the world in mathematics and science achievement by the year 2000), President Bush and the governors called for "decentralization of authority and decision-making responsibility to the school site, so that educators are empowered to determine the means for achieving the goals and to be held accountable for accomplishing them" ("'A Jeffersonian Compact':

The Statement by the President and Governors," 1989). The federal government might set the goals, but the question of how to achieve them was left to the states and their local districts. This summit led to the Goals 2000: Educate America Act that President Bill Clinton signed in 1994 (North Central Regional Educational Laboratory, 1994).

> *The federal government might set the goals, but the question of how to achieve them was left to the states and their local districts.*

By the year 2000, however, the United States had not come close to achieving any of its education goals. Leaving education in the hands of fifty states and more than fifteen thousand local school districts was not yet providing students with a world-class education.

Perhaps one of the reasons for the failure of the Goals 2000: Educate America Act was that few states had a process for monitoring student learning or holding schools accountable for that learning (Civic Impulse, n.d.b). Many states relied on nationally normed tests that placed students along a continuum of achievement rather than a criterion-referenced test designed to determine which students had met a designated proficiency level.

As of 2002, only nine states required all students in grades 3–8 to take a criterion-referenced test in English language arts, and only seven did so in mathematics (Aldeman, 2015). Most states looked at student performance as a whole rather than disaggregating data by particular groups of students, and only twenty-two states disaggregated high school graduation rates (Aldeman, 2015). At the beginning of the 21st century, if someone accused a school that its students were not learning, in most instances the charges would be dismissed for a lack of evidence. In response to this chaotic situation, the U.S. government stepped in.

No Child Left Behind Act

Within three days of assuming office in 2001, President George W. Bush called for the adoption of NCLB as his first legislative initiative. By December of that year, the law passed with overwhelming bipartisan support in both the Senate and House of Representatives—87 to 10 and 381 to 41, respectively (Civic Impulse, n.d.a). Its broad themes of additional funding for education, academic standards, accountability, civil rights, and school choice found widespread support in the early days of 2002.

NCLB signaled a major turning point in the effort to reform U.S. education by dramatically increasing the authority of the federal government in matters that had largely been left to the states. The Commission on No Child Left Behind (2007) described it as impacting education "more than any other federal education law in history" and a "bold step to accelerate progress in education and fulfill our promise to our nation's children" (p. 11).

NCLB aimed to replace this *laissez-faire* approach to education by establishing accountability with a capital *A*. While the French expression *laissez-faire* often describes free trade or other economic policies that allow individuals or nation-states to do as they wish, it described education well in the years before NCLB, when there was no national consensus on what students should know and be able to do. Only a few states, including Missouri (the Show-Me Standards) and Florida (the Sunshine State Standards), had established academic content standards and state tests, and the prevailing view was for *local control*, meaning each school district—indeed, each school and classroom— was left on its own to decide what an acceptable level of student performance should be.

NCLB mandated annual assessments in reading and mathematics in grades 3–8 and once in high school. Schools were required to report results separately by race, ethnicity, and other key demographic groups. They also were required to demonstrate adequate yearly progress and faced interventions and increasingly severe sanctions if they failed to do so.

If a school failed to make adequate yearly progress two years in a row, students in that school were allowed to transfer to another school in the district that was meeting standards, and the state would hold back 10 percent of the school's Title I money. Failure for a third year meant the school had to provide free tutoring services to students. Continued failure could lead to state interventions, such as closing the school, turning it into a charter school, taking control of the school, or using another turnaround strategy.

The Goals 2000 initiative established thirty-eight different factors to determine whether or not a school was failing under NCLB. A school's inability to meet the standard of any one of these thirty-eight factors meant the entire school was failing. By the year 2014, the inability of a single student to demonstrate proficiency on the mandated state test meant the school would be designated as failing. If educators did not improve student achievement, they would be subjected to increasingly punitive sanctions for failure to do so (U.S. Department of Education, 2003).

> *A school's inability to meet the standard of any one of these thirty-eight factors meant the entire school was failing.*

However, NCLB left the questions of which academic standards to adopt, which annual assessments to use, and what constituted proficiency on those assessments to each state to decide. So how did states respond? In too many cases, they lowered standards, adopted easier assessments, and set low benchmarks for proficiency in an effort to ensure their schools would look good to residents and avoid NCLB sanctions. Critics of the law described this phenomenon as an educational race to the bottom.

Within five years of the passage of NCLB, Michael Petrilli, a member of the Bush administration charged with overseeing this law, concluded that even though initially he had been a "true believer," he had "reluctantly come to the conclusion that NCLB as enacted is fundamentally flawed and probably beyond repair" (Thomas B. Fordham Institute, 2007). He lamented the fact that asking all states to reach universal proficiency by 2014 but allowing them to define proficiency as they saw fit had, inevitably, created a race to the bottom. He writes, "I can't pretend any longer that the law is 'working,' or that a tweak and a tuck would make it work" (Thomas B. Fordham Institute, 2007).

In 2009, the National Governors Association (NGA) and the Council of Chief State School Officers (CCSSO) proposed a plan to address the NCLB problems of lowered expectations—the Common Core State Standards.

Common Core State Standards

If states could agree to a set of national standards in mathematics and English language arts and on the assessments to monitor student achievement of those standards, they could promote greater academic rigor and a more accurate comparison of student achievement between states. Thus, the Common Core State Standards initiative was born, an initiative initially supported by forty-five states (NGA & CCSSO, 2010b).

Meanwhile, however, the stipulations of NCLB remained in effect, and each year as more and more schools failed to demonstrate adequate yearly progress, states petitioned the U.S. Department of Education under President Barack Obama's administration for waivers to avoid sanctions and allow them to pursue other avenues of school improvement. President Obama and Secretary of Education Arne Duncan used this opportunity to provide waivers only if states agreed to implement the Obama administration's education priorities, collectively known as RTTT.

According to the U.S. Department of Education (2009), the states agreed to include the following six priorities.

1. Work collaboratively with other states to adopt a common set of high-quality standards internationally benchmarked that ensure college and career readiness. (This stipulation was generally understood to mean that states must embrace the emerging Common Core State Standards.)

2. Join a consortium of states to administer rigorous assessments based on the internationally benchmarked standards.

3. Make student growth (or value-added testing) a factor in teacher and principal evaluations, including decisions regarding retention or removal of tenured and untenured teachers.

4. Make student growth a factor in a plan to provide additional compensation (merit pay) for effective teachers and principals.

5. Identify persistently low-performing schools (the bottom 5 percent in the state) and develop plans to either close or reconstitute them.

6. Provide alternative routes to certification for both teachers and principals.

RTTT offered federal funding to cash-starved states struggling to deal with the most dramatic recession since the Great Depression of the 1930s. However, to receive the funds, states had to compete with one another to demonstrate their willingness to embrace RTTT requirements. Education policies states had been reluctant to enact and Congress had been unwilling to mandate soon became implemented through multibillion-dollar carrots coming precisely at a time when school systems most needed federal funds. Two-thirds of the states changed their laws on teacher evaluation, half the states declared student test scores would be included in teacher evaluations, and eighteen weakened tenure protections (Goldstein, 2014). While NCLB might punish schools, RTTT provided the tools to punish individual teachers and principals. Finally, it was time to assess these reform efforts and ask, "How are they working?"

> *While NCLB might punish schools, RTTT provided the tools to punish individual teachers and principals.*

Assessment of Reform Efforts

Educators are familiar with the reform strategies that have swept over them since the passage of NCLB—launching test-based accountability that ensured every public school would eventually be designated as failing, increasing the availability of vouchers so students could abandon public schools, taking steps to make it easier to fire educators and replace them with people with no education background, insisting on teacher evaluations based on standardized test scores, reconstituting schools, closing schools, and providing merit pay. All this was done to promote the goals of ensuring U.S. schools would become the highest-performing schools in the world and improving poor and minority students' achievement.

After many years of experience with these punitive strategies, it is fair to ask, "How has that worked for us?" In Rick's book *In Praise of American Educators: And How They Can Become Even Better* (DuFour, 2015), he makes the case that these reforms failed. He is not alone in arriving at this conclusion. The National Center for Education and the Economy concludes, "There is no evidence that it (the reform agenda) is contributing anything to improved student performance, much less the improved performance of the very low-income and minority students for which it was in the first instance created" (Tucker, 2014, p. 2).

Similarly, the National Education Policy Center writes, "A sober and honest look at the effects of the No Child Left Behind Act reveals a broad consensus among researchers that this system is at best ineffective and at worst counter-productive" (Welner & Mathis, 2015, p. 7).

The number of U.S. students scoring below proficient on the Programme for International Student Assessment (PISA) exam has remained flat since the early 2000s (Sparks, 2016), and other indicators of student achievement were rising faster in the decade before NCLB than the decade after its passage (FairTest, 2015). Not a single state came anywhere near the NCLB goals, and none of the highest-performing nations in the world were using any of the reform strategies imposed on U.S. public schools. The efforts of the federal government to make student achievement in the United States the highest in the world have clearly failed.

> *Not a single state came anywhere near the NCLB goals, and none of the highest-performing nations in the world were using any of the reform strategies imposed on U.S. public schools.*

Since the founding of public schools, there has been a history of fierce independence. While many European nations settled on national curricula, the colonies were as independent about education as they were about governance. Despite calls for education reform from leaders such as Thomas Dewey in the late 19th century and *A Nation at Risk* in the late 20th century, education remained firmly within the control of local and state governments. The 21st century ushered in sixteen years of a dramatic increase in the influence of the national government on education policy, first with No Child Left Behind and then with Race to the Top. While there was a bipartisan support for the legislation, and a nearly universal pursuit of the dollars attached to it, the price of federal control ultimately exceeded its value. Thus, in December 2015, a bipartisan majority of Congress passed the Every Student Succeeds Act, signed by President Obama, while Republican senators and members of congress stood behind him. This legislation appeared to turn the tide of federal control of education and a range of matters, from testing to curriculum to teacher evaluation, back to the states. In the next chapter, we consider the implications of this important law.

CHAPTER 2

The Passage
of ESSA

B y the time NCLB came up for reauthorization in 2007, Democrats and Republicans in Congress, who could agree on little else, were united in their dislike of the law. More and more schools were deemed failing. Conservatives were concerned about federal overreach in a matter they felt should be reserved for the states. Liberals were concerned that the NCLB provision that endorsed and funded the creation of more charter schools, many of which are run by private companies, and the inevitability of every school failing represented an attempt to abandon public education and privatize schooling. They also objected to the fact that the law was never fully funded. But despite common distaste for the law, politicians on the right and left could not agree on a plan for amending it.

As mentioned in chapter 1, the Obama administration tied approval of state petitions for waivers from NCLB sanctions to plans that reflected its agenda for education reform. This tactic only magnified the opposition of those against any attempt of the federal government to influence K–12 education.

Even though the idea of Common Core State Standards and national assessments originated with U.S. governors and chief state school administrators, conservatives disapproved of the U.S. Department of Education's efforts to tie those initiatives to state waivers. The department's insistence that teacher evaluation, retention, and compensation be tied to a single test that purported to demonstrate a teacher's impact on a student's learning was attacked by teacher unions and denounced by almost all education assessment experts.

Yet, year after year, Congress was unable to come up with an alternative to NCLB and RTTT. Democrats wanted to remove test results as the way to evaluate teacher effectiveness and guarantees that the law would protect racial minorities and children of poverty, the targets of the original ESEA in 1965. Republicans wanted states and local districts to be free to establish their own education policies with little or no federal intervention or influence (Huetteman & Rich, 2015).

Finally, in 2015, the two parties were able to agree on a compromise bill with overwhelming bipartisan support—85 to 12 in the Senate and 359 to 64 in the House of Representatives—which later became ESSA.

Democrats were pleased that states would still require schools to test all students in grades 3–8 and once in high school in mathematics, language arts, and science. They also were pleased that schools would continue to report student scores by subgroups, so student performance in general could not mask the underachievement of a particular group; states would no longer be required to use test results in evaluating teachers; and test scores would become less of a focus under the new bill (Severns, 2015).

Republicans were pleased that the new law dramatically reduced the role of the federal government in K–12 education. In a thinly disguised rebuke of former Secretary of Education Duncan, one of the major changes under the law is a reduction of the influence any secretary of education might have on policy. The secretary is expressly prohibited from the following.

- Influencing the adoption of any particular standards
- Impacting the nature of assessments
- Prescribing any aspect of the accountability system
- Advocating for specific school supports or improvement strategies

- Prescribing any aspect of educator evaluation systems as measures of effectiveness

The federal government could no longer prescribe goals or punishments. States assumed authority for establishing their own standards, tests, goals, accountability systems, and what to do with schools that underperformed (Klein, 2016a).

ESSA is a clear departure from federal laws and regulations that extended the reach of the federal government in K–12 education. While NCLB required states to have academic standards and accompanying tests, and RTTT explicitly provided financial incentives for grant recipients to adopt the Common Core State Standards, ESSA categorically prohibits sanctions and penalties on matters involving standards, curriculum, assessments, and teacher evaluations. Senator Lamar Alexander, a sponsor of the legislation, said that it restored "to states, school districts, classroom teachers, and parents the responsibility for deciding what to do about improving student achievement" (Rubin, 2015). *The New York Times* agreed and characterized the law as a restoration of local control of schooling (Huetteman & Rich, 2015).

> *ESSA is a clear departure from federal laws and regulations that extended the reach of the federal government in K–12 education.*

The Wall Street Journal described the law as representing "the largest devolution of federal control" to the states in twenty-five years (Wong, 2015). The Brown Center on Education Policy, however, bemoaned the federal retreat from U.S. classrooms and the fact that the federal government's fifty-year effort of trying to improve educational opportunities for poor and minority students had accomplished so little (Shober, 2015). The Brown Center, part of the Brookings Institution in Washington, DC, notes that the timing of ESEA in 1965 was closely related to civil rights legislation, and that local states and school districts had not distinguished themselves in education policies that benefitted all students. The center is, therefore, alarmed at what it regarded as a retreat from federal responsibility that is implied in ESSA.

In essence, ESSA includes some old ideas from NCLB but combines them with improved ideas, giving the states more flexibility.

Something Old and Something New

NCLB required every state to adopt academic standards in reading, mathematics, and science. It also stipulated annual testing in reading and mathematics of all students in grades 3–8 and once in high school. Teachers were asked to administer science tests once in grades 3–5, once in grades 6–8, and once in high school. In addition, schools were required to issue an annual report card on the achievement of all students as well as subgroups, such as special education, racial minorities, English learners, and children living in poverty (Klein, 2015b).

ESSA continues the NCLB policies of annual testing and reporting but also expands subgroup reports on test scores and graduation rates to include students who are foster children, homeless, or from military families (Klein, 2016a). Gone are the federal government mandates for annual yearly progress and stipulated penalties for failure to meet proficiency targets. States are free to set their long-term achievement goals, measurements of progress, and what consequences, if any, they apply to a school for poor performance.

Gone too is the idea that governments should determine a school's failure or success solely from student performance on a single comprehensive test. Under ESSA, states can opt to administer shorter-interim assessments throughout the year that result in a single score rather than one comprehensive test. They also can choose to substitute nationally recognized tests, such as the SAT or ACT, for their high school state achievement test.

Additionally, states can include factors beyond test scores to assess the quality of a school. Schools must use at least three academic indicators, such as student proficiency on state tests, student growth on state tests, and English language proficiency. At the high school level, schools must also include graduation rates. But states can include other factors, such as student engagement, faculty engagement, school climate and safety, access to and completion of advanced coursework, postsecondary readiness, or whatever else the state feels is significant to assess the quality of a school. No longer will schools be labeled as failing if they miss an achievement target for a single group of students.

States can take a more holistic look to determine whether schools are succeeding or failing.

Every three years, the states must report on Title I schools among the lowest 5 percent, high schools with graduation rates of less than 67 percent, and Title I schools with one or more low-performing subgroups among the lowest 5 percent. Local districts are responsible for providing the plan and assistance to improve these low-performing schools. If the district is unable to help these schools meet improvement criteria, the state is required to step in and implement more rigorous action.

States can take a more holistic look to determine whether schools are succeeding or failing.

NCLB's mandate that classrooms be staffed with highly qualified teachers has been replaced by a provision that all teachers working in Title I-A programs must meet their state's certification and licensure requirements, and poor and minority students in schools receiving the funds must not be taught by ineffective teachers at higher rates than other students. The controversial RTTT stipulations that teacher evaluations include evidence of student growth on a standardized achievement test and support merit pay cease to exist, although states may elect to make them part of their teacher evaluation process. Because in many states these provisions required legislative action to apply for RTTT grants, it will take legislative action to reverse the policy.

An Opportunity for Change

Senator Alexander painted a rosy picture of the impact of the law when he stated, "What I believe is that when we take the handcuffs off, we'll unleash a whole flood of innovation and ingenuity classroom by classroom, state by state, that will benefit children" (Klein, 2016b).

We contend that Senator Alexander's prediction (which sounds eerily like President H. W. Bush's 1989 assurances of the benefits of decentralizing authority and empowering each school site) represents the triumph of optimism over experience. As we referenced earlier, throughout most U.S. education history, districts have been unencumbered by standards, expectations, and accountability from their state departments of education. It is difficult to establish evidence that this *laissez-faire* approach to education led to high levels of student learning. In fact, President Reagan's National Commission on Excellence in Education concluded that this approach had put the entire nation at risk.

ESSA does not present states and local districts with a panacea, but it does present them with an opportunity and a challenge.

We have already described the failure of the federal government to improve U.S. schooling, and we are not advocating that the federal government become the major force in education. We are simply pointing out that there is no guarantee that delivering more authority to the states will improve U.S. education. ESSA does not present states and local districts with a panacea, but *it does present them with an opportunity and a challenge.*

Whether the passage of ESSA represents a step forward or backward in the effort to ensure high levels of learning for *all* students depends on how states respond to their new autonomy for overseeing their own school-improvement processes. If states return to the low-accountability, *laissez faire* oversight that typically preceded NCLB, there will be no sense of academic pressure to improve student achievement.

Schools that can avoid the bottom 5 percent of performance on state assessments and the bottom 5 percent of Title I schools on subgroup performance, and can help more than two-thirds of their high school students graduate, may have little external incentive to improve. If, on the other hand, states merely create their own versions of the punitive strategies of NCLB and RTTT, there is no reason to expect different results from those of the No Child Left Behind Era of 2001–2016.

There is, however, an opportunity for states to move school reform in a much more promising direction if leaders adopt and sustain a new mindset regarding what is required to help students learn at higher levels. In chapter 3, we address that mindset and strategies proven to be most successful in improving student achievement around the world.

CHAPTER 3

How States Can
Respond to ESSA

The message of NCLB and RTTT to educators was not subtle—*improve or else.* The highest-performing countries, including Finland, Singapore, and South Korea, recognize that a school is only as good as the people within it, and therefore, improvement efforts should be based not on threats, but on building the capacity of educators to achieve the desired results. Furthermore, these countries have consistently turned to the PLC process as the key strategy for capacity building (Barber & Mourshed, 2009).

Responding to ESSA will require a fundamental shift from compliance to collaboration. In this chapter, we consider what states and local school districts should embrace in order to establish a culture of effective collaboration, and we also suggest what states and districts should stop doing. While no research is perfect, including in physics, chemistry, and biology, the preponderance of the evidence in education is clear about what does and does not work. The following sections seek to elevate evidence over opinion in implementing education policies.

A New Mindset

If states pursue this new direction, they must abandon the thinking that led to failed reforms and embrace a new mindset regarding the most promising strategies to improve their schools. That mindset must include the following five strategies.

1. Support teacher collaboration along with widely dispersed leadership.

2. Establish clarity of purpose regarding collaboration.

3. Provide ongoing feedback to help educators address strengths and weaknesses.

4. Create conditions allowing educators to succeed at what they are asked to do.

5. Protect educators from other initiatives while they improve the PLC process.

We discuss each of these strategies in detail in the following sections.

Support Teacher Collaboration and Widely Dispersed Leadership

A primary obstacle to improving student achievement since the 1970s is the fact that U.S. educators work in isolation rather than in collaborative teams. States must create the expectation that the fundamental school structure consists of collaborative teams that take collective responsibility for student learning, rather than the isolated classroom teacher.

States must create the expectation that the fundamental school structure consists of collaborative teams that take collective responsibility for student learning, rather than the isolated classroom teacher.

Education policymakers and educators themselves must recognize that the other tasks of teaching and learning—planning, pacing, assessing, examining evidence of student work, providing feedback, reflecting, and adjusting instruction—are essential and are best accomplished in collaborative teams rather than in isolation. States must loosen their regulations and fixation on the number of instruction minutes to allow and also support time for educators to regularly collaborate in teams, so that they can continually expand their content knowledge, hone their skills, and learn with and from their colleagues. Jon Saphier, Mary Ann Haley-Speca, and Robert Gower (2008) point out:

> There is more to good teaching than skill, but there is no good teaching without it . . . skillful teachers are learners. . . . Skillful teachers constantly reach out to colleagues with an assertive curiosity that says, "I don't know it all. No one does or ever will, but I am always growing, adding to my knowledge and skills and effectiveness." To skillful teachers, that openness and reaching out is an important element of professionalism. (p. 2)

The PLC process guarantees all teachers frequent and learning-focused access to their collaborative team members with whom they share both content and students.

Principals play a key role in transforming traditional schools into high-performing PLCs, but no one person has the expertise, energy, and influence to bring about that transformation. The PLC process creates opportunities for widely dispersed leadership. Influential teachers can serve on a guiding coalition with the principal to lead the process. Schools can create a team leader position for each team and provide the training and support to help these individuals lead their colleagues in the collaborative process. Opportunities for situational leadership arise when evidence of student learning from common assessments reveals that a teacher on the team has strengths in teaching a skill or concept that he or she can share with team members. States can support principal and teacher leader training and provide incentives for educators to take on greater leadership responsibilities.

Establish Clarity of Purpose Regarding Collaboration

Simply providing educators with time to collaborate will do nothing to improve student achievement unless collaboration focuses on the right work. If team members use collaborative time to commiserate, share war stories, debate personal preferences, or question the purpose of why they are meeting at all, neither teachers nor students benefit.

Simply providing educators with time to collaborate will do nothing to improve student achievement unless collaboration focuses on the right work.

Fortunately, as Rick (DuFour, 2015) stresses in *In Praise of American Educators*, there is no mystery regarding what represents the right work.

- Teams must ensure members work interdependently to achieve common SMART goals (strategic and specific, measurable, attainable, results oriented, and time bound; Conzemius & O'Neill, 2014) for which each member is mutually accountable.

- Teams must establish and implement a guaranteed and viable curriculum, unit by unit, that ensures all students have access to the same knowledge, skills, and dispositions, regardless of their assigned teacher. Teams must establish common pacing for each unit and also the criteria to use in judging the quality of student work.

- Teams must embrace an assessment process that includes ongoing checks for student understanding almost minute by minute while teaching, and at least one or more team-developed common formative assessment for each unit of instruction.

- Teams must use the evidence of student learning from common formative assessments to identify the following.

  - Students who need additional time and support for learning

  - Highly proficient students who would benefit from an extension of their learning

  - Strengths and weaknesses of individual team members that the team can address as a whole

  - Areas of student learning for which the team is unable to bring students to proficiency; therefore, members require assistance and support in developing new strategies for teaching those skills and concepts

- The school must provide time during the regular school day when struggling students receive additional time and support for learning in a way that is systematic, diagnostic, directive, and does not remove the student from new direct instruction.

States are well positioned to support the work of collaborative teams in many ways. States might choose to do the following.

- Adopt state standards that represent what is truly essential for students to know and be able to do at each grade level, rather than providing the traditional curriculum catchall that covers too much content with too little depth

- Make available well-designed assessment items, examples of performance assessments, and sample rubrics for each subject and grade level

- Provide examples of high-quality student work at each grade level in different content areas

- Support the technology to help teams get ready access to information about student learning and extend their collaboration with other educators beyond school walls

- Establish a network of electronic teams for singleton teachers to connect with others who teach their subject or grade level

- Create video libraries of effective instructional strategies for key concepts in different grade levels and courses

- Provide incentives for schools at all levels to use the PLC process to address the ESSA teacher-engagement-quality indicator

- Help identify schools and districts that serve as high-performing models of the PLC process

- Most important, provide a steady, consistent, coherent, and unrelenting message about the collaborative teams' work because clarity precedes competence in doing that work

Applying the PLC process consistently over time is key to a positive impact on student achievement. In a performance review of 196 schools with more than 750,000 students participating in the PLC at Work process, Douglas finds that schools involved in this PLC work for more than seven to ten years dramatically outperform schools that had only been participating for three years (Reeves, 2015). Additionally,

Applying the PLC process consistently over time is key to a positive impact on student achievement.

schools committed to consistent implementation of PLCs over time experienced three to five times the growth in reading, mathematics, and science when compared to schools involved for shorter periods of time (Reeves, 2015).

No matter how good the intentions of ESSA authors and implementers, however, a long-term commitment to effective practice remains elusive when leadership turnover at the state and district levels virtually guarantees changing priorities. The evidence is clear that consistency and focus are essential for effective PLC implementation, and future success depends on avoiding the typical fad chasing that has dominated education reform throughout the last half of the 20th century and well into the 21st.

We doubt that a change in state or district leadership would lead successive leaders to stop taking attendance or disregard school safety. Commitments to equity are long-established values that should not waver based on political philosophy or party affiliation. Those are consistent priorities no matter the political persuasion of those in charge of education policy. Similarly, the consistent implementation of PLCs is a matter of principle, value, and safety. When student achievement is higher, every jurisdiction benefits from lower health-care expenditures, higher levels of employment, greater tax revenues, and fewer resources allocated to the criminal justice system (Amos, 2016). The stakes could not be higher.

Commitments to equity are long-established values that should not waver based on political philosophy or party affiliation.

Provide Ongoing Feedback to Help Educators Address Strengths and Weaknesses

RTTT encouraged states to place more emphasis on improving schools by having principals supervise and evaluate individual teachers into higher performance. This strategy suffers from several faulty assumptions, such as the following.

- Principals, who already report being overwhelmed by their job responsibilities, can devote themselves to the time-intensive task of supporting each staff member through multiple observations and evaluation cycles.

- Principals have the pedagogical and content expertise to provide valuable feedback to teachers from different grade levels and subject areas.

- Principals make recommendations to persuade teachers to change their instructional practices.

But the biggest fallacy in this strategy is the assumption that improving individual teachers' instruction creates high-performing schools. A robust body of research indicates that school leaders hoping to improve their schools should spend their time and energy in areas other than teacher evaluation (Murphy, Hallinger, & Heck, 2013). Michael Fullan (2010) warns strategies that focus on improving individuals, no matter how good, never result in widespread change. Strengthening collective capacity, he advises, "is the *sina qua non* of system reform" (p. 71).

Common sense should apply here. Which is more likely to convince an educator to change his or her practice? Is it being observed by a supervisor who offers a subjective assessment of the teacher's performance four of five times per year? Or is it meeting with colleagues at least weekly to agree on what students must learn, creating assessments on whether or not they have learned it, and then examining transparent evidence of student learning with their peers to determine instructional strengths and weaknesses? Teachers do not need a principal to judge them—they need two things: (1) a process that provides ongoing feedback on the impact of their teaching so they can make adjustments and (2) a support system of colleagues to help them. States should ensure that every teacher has access to that feedback and support.

Create Conditions Allowing Educators to Succeed at What They Are Asked to Do

The prevailing assumption of U.S. school reform efforts has been that educators must be threatened with increasing punishment in order to put forth the effort to improve schools. As Michael Barber and Mona Mourshed (2007) point out, "One cannot give what one does not have" (p. 16), regardless of the threats. States have an opportunity to adopt a very different mindset based on the notion that the challenge of improving schools is fundamentally a challenge to build the collective capacity of educators.

The challenge for states is to ask, "How can state policymakers, including legislatures and state departments of education, help support educators in building their collective capacity so they can succeed in improving student achievement, effective teaching, and leadership?" The following five points provide examples of that support.

1. Influencing the adoption of any particular standards

2. Impacting the nature of assessments

3. Prescribing any aspect of the accountability system

4. Advocating for specific school supports or improvement strategies

5. Prescribing any aspect of educator evaluation systems as measures of effectiveness

States also should have systems for providing districts and schools with specific training and support. In Canada, the provincial government of Ontario provides a great example of fully supported systemwide reform. If an Ontario elementary school is unable to help at least 75 percent of its students meet the provincial standard on its assessments, it becomes part of the Ontario Focused Intervention Plan (OFIP; Fullan, 2014; Ontario Ministry of Education, 2014).

States also should have systems for providing districts and schools with specific training and support.

Rather than resorting to sanctions, the program takes a capacity-building approach, operating under the assumption that educators must be the force for change, and the ministry must help build the collective capacity of educators to overcome their challenges (DuFour & Fullan, 2013).

OFIP provides support for on-site professional learning in the following ways.

- Offering advice

- Sharing research into effective practices

- Creating structures to encourage collaborative inquiry into practice problems

- Gathering and analyzing data to identify student learning needs

- Monitoring progress

- Building networking opportunities with other schools of similar demographics that have been successful in overcoming their challenges

- Funding a $15,000 stipend to provide the staff with release time for planning, monitoring, reflecting, and integrating learning into classroom practice

A provincial capacity-building team also provides ongoing consulting services directly to the school (Ontario Ministry of Education, 2014).

OFIP schools must complete a needs assessment, develop an action plan, engage the faculty in a school-based PLC, and participate in formal and informal learning opportunities. When the program began in 2003–2004, the Ontario Education Quality and Accountability Office (EQAO) identified 780 elementary schools in need of assistance. By 2014, the number had shrunk to sixty-three, even though the EQAO had raised the required prerequisite standard of achievement (Ontario Ministry of Education, 2014).

Furthermore, the improvement rate for OFIP schools has exceeded provincial averages throughout the program's history (Ontario Ministry of Education, 2014). This school-improvement approach led to Ontario consistently scoring twenty or more points above the Organisation for Economic Co-operation and Development (OECD) average on all three assessed areas of the PISA exam: (1) reading literacy, (2) mathematical literacy, and (3) scientific literacy. The OECD average is:

> The mean of the data values for all OECD countries for which data are available or can be estimated. The OECD average can be used to see how a country compares on a given indicator with a typical OECD country. (OECD, 2005, p. 144)

Protect Educators From Other Initiatives While They Improve the PLC Process

Districts that demonstrate the greatest progress in student learning have a shared sense of purpose, a clear direction, explicit commitments from educators regarding the steps they will take to support the collective effort to improve the school, and, very important, a few very focused goals.

Some states use a school-improvement model that calls on struggling schools to establish goals for ninety-five different aspects of effective schooling, with quarterly updates on progress. This approach is a recipe for disaster and almost certainly guarantees that educators will devote more time to completing paperwork than engaging in a meaningful process to improve student achievement.

Districts that demonstrate the greatest progress in student learning have a shared sense of purpose, a clear direction, explicit commitments from educators regarding the steps they will take to support the collective effort to improve the school, and, very important, a few very focused goals. As Michael Fullan and Joanne Quinn (2016) wisely observe:

> The problem is not the absence of goals in districts and schools today but the presence of too many that are ad hoc, unconnected, and ever-changing. They are too often fragmented and so people see them as discrete demands with little or no connection to the work. . . . The solution lies in developing limited goals, persisting, and avoiding distracters. The best leaders use goals to establish continuous, focused direction. (pp. 20–21)

Policy prescriptions are easier than pulling the plug. That is why nearly every school we have encountered is buried under a series of well-intentioned initiatives. Some of these initiatives should simply end.

What States Should Stop Doing

In order to make available time and resources for effective collaboration, as well as to avoid the cultural impediments that undermine collaboration, we offer some ideas for what states should stop doing.

Offering Merit Pay and Basing Teacher Evaluation on Test Scores

In light of the failure of NCLB and RTTT sanction-driven strategies, states should abandon both the *carrot* (merit pay) and *stick* (punishment and dismissal) approach to school improvement and focus instead on policies that develop the capacity of educators to solve problems in their schools. For example, ESSA no longer requires the use of value-added testing or growth in student test scores in individual teacher evaluations. No state should continue with this practice. The American Statistical Association (2014), Richard J. Shavelson and his colleagues (2010), the Educational Testing Service (Braun, 2005), and the Rand Corporation (McCaffrey, Lockwood, Koretz, & Hamilton, 2003), among others, cite it as an inaccurate, invalid process for individual teacher evaluation. This flawed process results in widely varying evaluations from year to year and assumes that a single teacher is responsible for the learning of a group of students.

Furthermore, in our estimation and experience, more than two-thirds of teachers teach nontested grades and subjects. The teachers in grades 3–8 account for six grades out of thirteen (from kindergarten through twelfth grade). And the time they devote to the tested subjects accounts for at most half of a school day. Therefore, at most 25 percent of teachers and teaching time is devoted to tested subjects in tested grades. District attempts to demand teacher evaluations based on test scores for these teachers often border on the absurd.

ESSA also no longer requires or endorses merit pay for teachers. The idea of merit pay is not new. It has been repeatedly tried and failed since the early 1900s in the United States. Organizational theorists Jeffrey Pfeffer and Robert I. Sutton (2006) describe the push for merit pay as total nonsense. They write:

> You don't have to read the evidence from literally decades of research to spot the problems with merit pay for schoolteachers. That evidence shows that merit-pay plans seldom last longer than five years and that merit pay consistently fails to improve student performance. The very logic of merit pay for teachers suggests that it won't do what it is intended to do. (p. 23)

As Fullan (2010) asserts emphatically, "I repeat, no research exists that demonstrates widespread benefits derive from merit pay" (p. 84). Furthermore, pitting teachers against each other in a battle for merit pay works against the collaborative culture and collective responsibility for student learning that characterizes highly effective schools. If states make decisions using compelling research and overwhelming evidence, they will abandon merit pay and teacher evaluations based on student test scores. Instead, states will focus on policies that build the capacity of educators to meet their school's challenges.

> *Pitting teachers against each other in a battle for merit pay works against the collaborative culture and collective responsibility for student learning that characterizes highly effective schools.*

Thinking of Time for Student Learning as Fixed Rather Than Variable

In most states, the designers of accountability systems presume that students have the same amount of time and same level of support to develop proficiency in the intended outcomes—for example, 180 days of school and 310 minutes of instruction each day. This instruction often occurs in a classroom with twenty-five to thirty-five students, each of whom receive roughly the same level of attention and support from the teacher each day.

The problem with this approach is that if time and support are constants, the variable is always learning. Some students may master a standard after three weeks of instruction, but others may need four. Some students demonstrate proficiency in a large-group setting, but others need more intensive small-group support.

Any state that hopes to have students learn at high levels should challenge its schools to answer the question, "How does your school respond at the end of an instructional unit when it is evident that some students have not learned?" Until a school has a systematic plan to provide struggling students with additional time and support for learning, those students will continue to be subjected to an education lottery in which the response to their struggles depends almost entirely on the randomness of their assigned teacher.

Focusing Exclusively on Summative Assessments

Under NCLB and RTTT, schools were evaluated based on a single summative test that yielded dichotomous results. The school was either passing or failing. A student was either proficient or not proficient. The tests typically provided little insight as to individual student strengths or weaknesses or the specific skills he or she might be lacking.

Rick Stiggins (2014), the founder of the Assessment Training Institute and former test development director for ACT, identifies some of the limitations of these annual summative assessments.

- Time restraints for testing means it is impossible to measure all key instructional areas students should master, so many key targets are not tested at all. Furthermore, areas that are tested cannot include enough items focused on any one learning target to support a judgment about student mastery of that target.

- If the test is limited to assessing the knowledge and skills of a particular grade level, it imposes an artificial ceiling because extremely capable students aren't allowed to demonstrate learning far beyond the grade-level content.

- To maximize efficiency and minimize costs, test developers have traditionally relied on multiple-choice assessments that don't address such 21st century skills as complex reasoning; oral and written communication skills; or the ability to create complex, achievement-related products. If teachers devote time to these important skills not addressed on the standardized test, a portion of the teacher's impact is effectively ignored.

- The tests are closed book, demanding recall of information; whereas in the information age, a student's ability to seek out, retrieve, and evaluate pertinent information to answer a question or solve a problem is an essential skill. Furthermore, standardized tests are typically timed and thus reward speed. The fact that a student who is a slow reader has time run out before getting to certain questions does not necessarily mean he or she doesn't know the answers.

- The time lapse between students taking the test and teachers receiving the results makes it an ineffective instrument for informing either the teacher or the student about content or skills that warrant additional attention.

There is a place for summative assessments, and ESSA continues the requirement that every student in grades 3–8 be tested each year in mathematics and reading, and that high school students be tested once. ESSA does allow states to administer shorter-interim assessments throughout the year that result in a single score rather than one comprehensive test, but the logistics of this option are unclear.

What is clear, however, is the benefit of educators using ongoing formative assessment in the classroom each day, and team-developed common formative assessments at least once for each unit of instruction. W. James Popham (2011) writes:

> We now have available about four decades' worth of empirical evidence attesting to the instructional dividends of the formative-assessment process. Indeed, when one considers several recent reviews of research regarding the classroom formative-assessment process, it is clear that the process works, it can produce whopping gains in students' achievement.

We are not suggesting that states create a series of tests and designate them as *formative*. It is the way educators use results rather than the test itself that determines if a test is formative. If educators use the test merely to assign grades, it is *summative*. If educators use the test to gain information about students who are struggling and where to go next with instruction, as well as inform students regarding where they need help to become proficient, it is *formative*.

We are suggesting that states emphasize the importance of formative assessment, provide training in the use of effective formative assessment, and create assessment item banks for grade-specific standards that teacher teams could access when developing their own assessments. A balanced assessment program includes both formative and summative assessments and integrates a variety of assessment strategies, including selected response, open ended, performance based, and observation. State testing is decidedly unbalanced, relying almost exclusively on summative assessments composed of multiple-choice items. States committed to improving student learning should support districts in the effective use of formative assessments.

> *A balanced assessment program includes both formative and summative assessments and integrates a variety of assessment strategies, including selected response, open ended, performance based, and observation.*

Leaving Teacher Preparation Up to Institutions and Organizations

ESSA abandoned the NCLB stipulation that a "highly qualified" teacher must provide instruction in each core academic course. Under ESSA, teachers in schools receiving Title I funds need only fulfill their state's licensing requirements. The way that individuals prepare for the teaching profession, however, has been under attack since 2001.

In 1995, the Holmes Group, a coalition of deans of American graduate schools, issued the report *Tomorrow's Schools of Education*. The report criticizes shoddy teacher education programs characterized by a lack of quality control, enormous gaps between schools and the world of practice, instruction in outmoded conceptions of teaching and learning, the needless division between theory and practice, and poor student teacher field placement (Holmes Group, 1995). It calls for revolutionizing teacher preparation and offers recommendations for a curriculum that includes child development, subject-matter content, pedagogy, technology, classroom management, inquiry-based action research, and collaborative skills (Holmes Group, 1995). The Holmes Group (1995) cautions that its recommendations require classrooms and schools to be "thoughtfully organized as communities of learning" (p. vii).

More than a decade later, Columbia Teachers College former President Arthur Levine (2006) issued a report criticizing teacher education programs for a curriculum in disarray, disconnected faculty, low admission standards, insufficient quality control, huge disparities in instructional quality, and students with inadequate preparation. In 2013, the National Council on Teacher Quality concluded that teacher preparation programs are "an industry of mediocrity churning out first-year teachers with classroom management skills and content knowledge inadequate to thrive in classrooms with ever-increasing ethnic and socioeconomic student diversity" (Greenberg, McKee, & Walsh, 2013, p. 1). It decries the fact that only one-quarter of the programs' limited admissions is for students who had graduated in the top half of their class, and only 7 percent of the programs provide students with uniformly strong experiences (Greenberg et al., 2013).

More than 1,300 traditional institutions and a growing number of alternative certification programs provide pathways for the teaching profession in the United States (Mehta, 2013). Unlike high-performing countries such as Finland and Singapore, where teacher education programs provide a standard curriculum to all teaching candidates, in the United States, teacher training is left to institutions providing certification programs with little consistency regarding the knowledge and skills individuals must have to be an effective teacher. Until there is widespread agreement on what a beginning teacher must know and be able to do, teacher preparation programs will continue to be in disarray. States must work with higher education and K–12 educators to establish the intended outcomes of teacher preparation programs, a core curriculum to support the acquisition of those outcomes, and rigorous assessments to help determine whether teacher candidates have acquired the intended knowledge and skills.

> *Until there is widespread agreement on what a beginning teacher must know and be able to do, teacher preparation programs will continue to be in disarray.*

States should also take steps to ensure teachers have the content expertise to help students achieve at high levels. More than one-third of secondary school mathematics and English teachers do not have a major in the subjects they are teaching. Twenty-nine percent of secondary science teachers have no degree in science. If one takes into account science teachers who are teaching outside of their major (for example, a biology major assigned to teach chemistry), the figure climbs much higher (Gutowski & Rado, 2014). In urban settings, the percentage of educators teaching outside their majors climbs higher still (Ingersoll, 2007). No other industrialized country allows its teachers to teach subjects for which they are not highly trained (Tucker, 2011).

Finally, states should follow the lead of other high-performing countries in establishing financial incentives for the top third of high school graduates to enter the teaching profession. Annual U.S. college costs are nearly double the OECD average (OECD, 2014b). Those with a bachelor's degree carry an average debt of $29,000 (Carey, 2015). To repay that debt, a prospective U.S. teacher will earn 68 percent of the mean salary of other college graduates or 20 percent less than the OECD average (OECD, 2014a). To demonstrate their belief that the teacher is the most important factor in student learning, states should spend less time focused on driving people from the profession through evaluation processes, and more time recruiting and attracting high-achieving students into the profession.

In the next chapter, we describe in detail the practices, policies, systems, and mindset that constitute a high-performing PLC school. In subsequent chapters, we address how districts and states can leverage the language of ESSA to support every U.S. school in implementing the PLC process.

CHAPTER 4

One School's Response to ESSA

I n this chapter, we offer a detailed scenario of Anywhere High School, a high-performing Professional Learning Community at Work. Although Anywhere High School is a fictional place, the structures, practices, policies, and culture we describe in the following pages are closely linked to those of Adlai E. Stevenson High School in Lincolnshire, Illinois. Stevenson High School has been implementing the PLC process to drive continuous improvement since 1983. Visit www.allthingsplc .info under the Evidence of Effectiveness tab to find other real-world examples of PLC districts and schools at all levels.

Prior to visiting Anywhere High School, it is important that we learn a little about its history. What were the past structures, practices, and culture, and how are they different from their current reality today?

The History of Anywhere High School

Before becoming an exemplary PLC, Anywhere High School faced the same obstacles to change as schools around the world. Students, parents, teachers, and administrators were generally happy with how things were going. High-achieving students regularly won trophies, and a few star faculty members won state and national recognition. The school had endured more than one strategic planning process, each with a mission and vision that ran several paragraphs. But beneath this thin veneer of success lay a shaky foundation. Teachers worked largely in isolation, concealing both excellence and mediocrity. Administrators worked under an unwritten code of "We won't make you work too hard if you don't make us work too hard," so feedback and evaluation systems were sparse and nearly meaningless. Parent complaints were few and, when they arose, were dealt with quietly so challenges to the prevailing system were never used as a catalyst for effective change.

Ultimately, however, the group that became the guiding coalition brought data into the open, allowing them to say publicly what had previously been only discussed in whispers. Their conclusion: we're not as good as we think we are, and we're not nearly as good as we could be. It was not one big change, but scores of small changes that led to the imperative for collaboration that is the hallmark of Anywhere High School. Laying the groundwork for change requires the following three essential steps.

The first essential step is a commitment to evidence. Just as great teachers since Socrates challenge students to support their conclusions with well-reasoned arguments and evidence, faculty leaders began to challenge prevailing claims that "the kids are doing just fine." Internal evidence on achievement, attendance, tardiness, and discipline showed that there was substantial room for improvement. External evidence on everything from student physiology to effective instruction demonstrated a gap between best practices and time-honored traditions.

The first essential step is a commitment to evidence.

The second essential step is a commitment to collective wisdom and collaboration. Guiding coalition members asked, "How can we do better?" as well as, "Where are the most effective practices in our building that are buried underneath the superficiality of average school performance?" This inquiry was not a witch hunt, but a treasure hunt. The goal was not to threaten and intimidate colleagues but identify and promote excellence wherever they found it, from an algebra class to the athletic field, and from American government to the drama club. Their commitment was to rebuild the foundation from the inside out, not by inundating their colleagues with externally driven initiatives.

The second essential step is a commitment to collective wisdom and collaboration.

The third essential step is a focus on results. Parts of the school, like the state champion track team, had a long history of a results orientation, with students and coaches using feedback during every practice to improve performance. Other parts of the school had responses to data ranging from resistance to neglect. Thanks to this focus on results, more and more meetings among faculty members included a clear contrast between where the school was and where it aspired to be. What had been vague goals slowly became SMART goals, and what had been lofty but ambiguous visions became crystal clear. The groundwork for change at Anywhere High School was not the result of a meeting or an inspirational speech, but rather as the result of leadership from inside the school establishing and maintaining a relentless commitment to improvement.

> *The third essential step is a focus on results.*

Upon entering Anywhere High School today, visitors see the school's mission statement posted throughout the building: *Help all students achieve the high levels of learning required for success in college or post-secondary training.* While there is nothing unusual about a school presenting its mission statement, what is striking about this school is the lengths it takes to articulate the specific conditions to fulfill its mission, the collective commitments of the administration and staff to bring those conditions to life in the school, and the specific schoolwide goals being monitored to mark progress toward fulfilling the mission.

The school has a guiding coalition, or leadership team, which includes the principal, a representative from every department, and the union president. The guiding coalition and the school staff as a whole make a concerted effort to ensure all new staff members are aware of the mission, vision, collective commitments, and goals that drive the daily work of the school. (Visit **go.SolutionTree.com/PLCbooks** for the free reproducible "The Foundation of Anywhere High School.") They specifically design interview questions to determine the degree to which the expectations and beliefs of potential candidates align with the foundation. (Visit **go.SolutionTree.com/PLCbooks** for the free reproducible "Staff Interview Questions.") The contract new employees sign includes a list of commitments for teachers and administrators.

During an orientation session for new staff, a teacher leader stresses that the intent of the foundation is to ensure Anywhere High School is a purpose-driven rather than a program-driven school. As the teacher leader explains, "We constantly remind ourselves of the purpose we are serving, the school we are trying to create, the commitments we have made to create such a school, and the goals we are pursuing." The orientation concludes with a thorough review of the foundation document, examples of how it impacts day-to-day decisions, changes made to traditional procedures that do not align with the foundation, and opportunities to ask questions seeking clarification.

The guiding coalition stresses that the foundation does not emerge at some board of education retreat but instead is created by the faculty, administration, parents, and students. The board asks for the creation of a task force that includes representatives from each stakeholder group and also from the board of education. Members of the task force work together to clarify the school's mission, conditions that support that mission, commitments necessary to move the school forward, and the benchmark indicators that track progress.

The board charges the task force to build shared knowledge regarding the research base supporting improving schools, align its recommendations with that base, and help build consensus to support its conclusions. The entire faculty then engages in small-group discussions to review the recommendations and ultimately build strong consensus to endorse the task force's work. The board of education agrees to protect the staff from new initiatives for at least three years, so task force members can focus on aligning the structure and culture of the school with the foundation.

At least twice each year, every parent of a high school student receives a copy of the mission, vision, collective commitments, and goals.

The school is also transparent in sharing foundation content with the community. At least twice each year, every parent of a high school student receives a copy of the mission, vision, collective commitments, and goals. The school urges parents to contact the administration any time they feel the board of education, administration, or a staff member is not living up to the articulated commitments.

The school also creates a parent task force to explore what parents can do to support both their children and the collective effort to create an outstanding school. That task force studies the research on parent-school partnerships and develops a list of recommendations for all parents to consider. The task force sends the list to all parents every year to help them identify how they can be positive, contributing members of the collective effort to ensure their children's success. (Visit **go.Solution Tree.com/PLCbooks** for the free reproducible "Parent Commitments.")

When asked how ESSA impacts the school's practice, members of the guiding coalition agree that it has little impact. As one member explains, "We have a very strong, united sense of purpose in our school. It is that sense of purpose and not legislation that drives our work. We know if we live up to our purpose, we will exceed the requirements of any regulations."

Like the members of the guiding coalition, teachers throughout Anywhere High School are confident in their ability to help all students succeed at high levels because they no longer work in isolation. Their school is characterized by a collaborative culture in which educators take collective responsibility for the success of each student entrusted to them.

Anywhere High School has taken the following steps to ensure all students are learning at high levels.

Support a Collaborative Culture

It is evident that the fundamental structure and engine that drive the work of Anywhere High School is the collaborative team. The typical team structure includes all the teachers who teach the same course (such as the biology team, world history team, ninth-grade English team) and some interdisciplinary teams. For example, the eleventh-grade American studies team combines English and U.S. history teachers in an interdisciplinary approach to literature and history. Some teams are vertical. For

It is evident that the fundamental structure and engine that drive the work of Anywhere High School is the collaborative team.

example, all French teachers of French I through advanced placement (AP) French work together to build a strong program. Teachers in career education fields organize a team to promote project-based learning with an emphasis on critical thinking, problem solving, and collaboration. Team members agree to a common rubric for assessing student work, share results, and brainstorm ideas on how to improve student learning.

When do teams find time to collaborate? Initially, the school devoted all its professional development days to collaborative team time. When it became evident that this strategy was not providing sufficient time for teams to complete their work, the school adjusted its schedule to push back the start of classes one day each week so every teacher could have an additional hour of weekly collaborative time. The school then adjusted its daily schedule again by pushing back the start of the instructional day by thirty minutes. The starting time for teachers remains the same, but they begin each day with an hour of uninterrupted time. Teachers devote two mornings each week to team meetings, but teams meet more frequently if they choose to do so.

The board informs the entire community of the schedule and links it to American Academy of Pediatrics (2014) recommendations that middle and high schools should not start school before 8:30 a.m. so as not to deprive teenagers of much-needed sleep. The board also points out that the new schedule gives students more opportunities to meet with counselors and teachers when they need help. The school adopts the change without controversy.

> *The school clearly demonstrates its commitment to creating a collaborative culture by ensuring teacher teams have time to do the work they are asked to do.*

Finally, if any team feels it needs more time to work together, the principal arranges for substitutes to cover for team members the entire day so they have another major block of collaboration time. The school clearly demonstrates its commitment to creating a collaborative culture by ensuring teacher teams have time to do the work they are asked to do. The team leader also points out that the time issue is a good example of the school's approach to problem solving. When initial efforts to provide adequate time didn't work out as hoped, there were no recriminations. Instead, the board of education asked the task force to come up with better ideas.

As the team leader puts it, "We are all about continuous improvement. We fail forward. We are able to attack the problem again more intelligently because we learn from what works and what doesn't."

Provide Clarity Regarding the Work

What is most striking about the work of the teams in Anywhere High School is the purposefulness with which they approach their tasks. There is no confusion regarding what they need to accomplish and no evidence of off-task behavior. A team leader facilitates the work of each team. These leaders apply for their positions and are trained in group facilitation skills. They meet quarterly with the administration to identify any problems and brainstorm possible solutions to those problems. These meetings give team leaders an opportunity to share effective strategies.

> *What is most striking about the work of the teams in Anywhere High School is the purposefulness with which they approach their tasks.*

Members of the algebra team are preparing to teach a new unit on a Common Core State Standard in the Reasoning with Equations and Inequalities domain (REI.B.3), calling on students to "solve linear equations and inequalities in one variable, including equations with coefficients represented by letters" (NGA & CCSSO, 2010a, p. 65). Each member agrees this is an essential skill that all students need to be highly successful in algebra.

The team agrees to devote two weeks to the unit and designates the day to give their common formative assessment. Members then turn to the results of the previous year's common formative assessment on that skill as a reminder of how students performed. They identify questions that created problems for a large number of students and then discuss if they need to revise or replace the questions or brainstorm ideas on how to help students demonstrate greater proficiency. One team member helped nearly all his students meet the proficiency standard, so he takes the lead in discussing potential strategies. His colleagues listen attentively and take notes on his ideas.

The team then sets a SMART goal for the unit (Conzemius & O'Neill, 2014). The previous year, 82 percent of students demonstrated proficiency on the initial unit test. The team agrees it will work to get at least 87 percent of the students proficient on the initial unit test this year. Although educators sometimes use the acronym *SMART* to mean different things, this team uses the following definitions (DuFour et al., 2016).

- Strategic (aligned with the organization's goals) and specific
- Measureable
- Attainable
- Results oriented
- Time bound (specifying when the goal will be achieved)

The state decides to use the ACT exam as the high school test for mathematics. So, a part of the team's discussion for each unit is to analyze released sets of ACT questions to determine how that test assesses different mathematics skills. The team then integrates ACT-style questions into daily classroom practice as well as its common assessment at the end of the unit. Team members explain that as part of every lesson, they advise students, "So this is how the ACT may assess you on this skill. Let's see if you are comfortable answering a problem like this."

Do team members resent the state mandating the ACT exam? Surprisingly, they are very supportive of the test. As one teacher explains, "Our mission is to help our students reach the levels of learning required for success in college or postsecondary training. So we see a test like the ACT, which is designed to be a predictor of success in postsecondary learning, as very much aligned with what we are attempting to accomplish."

Another team member adds, "We really embrace the ACT as a way to help our students. Many colleges make admission decisions on the basis of class rank and scores from tests like the ACT or SAT. There is no way we can help 100 percent of our students graduate in the top quarter of the class. But with the ACT, we can help all our students achieve scores that demonstrate they can be successful in college or postsecondary training."

Members of the sophomore English team share their students' scores on a persuasive writing assignment using a modified Smarter Balanced Consortium rubric (www.smarterbalanced.org). Each member applies the rubric to his or her students' writing and brings the results to the meeting. Before the analysis begins, however, the team leader gives each team member a copy of the same student's essay to score individually using the agreed-on five-point rubric. When the team finishes, the team leader asks all members to present their scores at the same time. There is never a deviation greater than one in the scores. The team then talks about the feedback it would give the student who wrote the essay.

The team uses this practice after each writing assignment to ensure everyone is providing students with consistent scores and feedback. In their initial efforts, members were surprised to find that their scores varied greatly, even when they were attempting to adhere to the same rubric. As one team member explains, "We learned two things. First, we discovered that our rubric needed to be more descriptive and much less subjective. Second, we learned that we were not providing our students with reliable scores and feedback. So, we practice scoring papers every month until now the difference in our scoring is minimal."

> *The team uses this practice after each writing assignment to ensure everyone is providing students with consistent scores and feedback.*

After their scoring practice, the team leader uses a protocol to help members analyze the data (Visit **go.SolutionTree.com/PLCbooks** for the free reproducible "Data Analysis.") First, team members list students who are not proficient and will need additional time and support to improve their persuasive writing. They also identify students who have scored highly proficient and discuss strategies for enriching their classroom experience.

The team then turns to analyzing each teacher's student-achievement data. The team leader presents each teacher's scores in an easy-to-understand format. The students of a particular teacher performed very well in one aspect of their writing—elaboration of evidence. That teacher shares some of the strategies she feels contributed to the high achievement. She agrees when the team leader asks if she is willing to videotape a lesson on elaboration of evidence that the team could use at an upcoming meeting.

The team is open with the evidence of student learning and eager to hear suggestions.

Some team members readily acknowledge that their students have not performed well and ask their colleagues for strategies they might incorporate into their lessons. The team is open with the evidence of student learning and eager to hear suggestions. One of the team norms is that the team focuses on the practice, not the person. Good scores mean a teacher uses some good practices. However, bad scores don't mean a teacher is a bad educator; it means he or she needs to learn some new practices.

The final step in the team's protocol is to identify an area on the assessment where no team member achieved the intended results. On this assignment, the students' use of writing conventions is disappointing. The team agrees to make that the topic of its next meeting, and the team leader promises to invite the school's literacy coach to the discussion. Another team member says she will pose the question on how to improve writing conventions to her online network of English teachers. Another promises to explore an online program called No Red Ink (https://noredink.com) to help students become aware of and improve their writing conventions.

At the end of the meeting, the team recommits to be open to new instructional practices. "It's one of the commitments our entire faculty has made," the team leader explains. "We said we will seek out the most promising practices in support of student learning. To honor that commitment, we have to do more than just share our opinions. We have to be willing to constantly learn."

It is evident that the collaborative team process and its emphasis on sharing transparent evidence of student learning is a catalyst for continuous improvement.

It is evident that the collaborative team process and its emphasis on sharing transparent evidence of student learning is a catalyst for continuous improvement. Several teachers acknowledge that although the school does not use the results from team-developed common formative assessments in the formal evaluation process, no teacher wants to be viewed as a consistently low performer by his or her colleagues. Rather than relying on sanctions to drive improvement, this school creates positive peer pressure to improve teaching.

The teams seem very clear regarding their work. They didn't actually start that way at the beginning of the process due to a lack of leadership. Then, the principal had simply assigned them to teams and given them time to collaborate, and they floundered.

"I learned that just giving people time to collaborate won't improve student learning," he says. "The key to improvement is whether we collaborate about the *right* work. For us, the right work is ensuring all students have access to a guaranteed and viable curriculum focused on the most essential knowledge and skills, constantly monitoring evidence of student learning through formative assessment in the classroom each day and at least one common formative assessment in each unit, and then using evidence of student learning to better meet the needs of students and inform and improve our instruction."

At the beginning of every course, each student receives the same syllabus that stipulates the knowledge and skills to acquire as a result of the course. The syllabus also includes how the teacher will evaluate student proficiency and determine grades. The staff are committed to providing students with an equitable learning experience that includes ensuring *all* students have access to the same essential curriculum and that their learning is assessed consistently.

Teams do not, however, settle for general agreement on learning and assessment for their course. The school's collaborative team process evolves around four critical questions that teams must address at the beginning of every unit of instruction. The principal can ask any faculty member about the four critical questions and is confident every person will respond with the questions that drive his or her professional work. These four critical questions are as follows.

1. What knowledge, skills, and dispositions should every student acquire as a result of this unit, this course, or this grade level?

2. How will we know when each student has acquired the essential knowledge and skills?

3. How will we respond when some students do not learn?

4. How can we extend the learning for students who are already proficient?

The principal believes these questions provide teachers with clarity and focus. As he explains, "When each teacher knows exactly what students should learn and exactly how students will demonstrate their learning, the teacher can provide very purposeful instruction. The common assessments the teams use provide every teacher with important feedback on the proficiency of his or her students compared to all the other students who took that same assessment. By providing this basis of comparison, teachers don't just get data—they get information. If I give an assessment and discover 80 percent of students achieve proficiency, I have data, but I don't have information. If only 50 percent of the other students achieve proficiency, my 80 percent is stellar. But if 95 percent of the other students achieve proficiency, I can turn to my teammates for help with new strategies. So, we are committed to giving all teachers this timely feedback so they can share their strengths and address their weaknesses."

ESSA allows schools to provide evidence of teacher engagement as one of its quality indicators. The combination of task forces to address problems and the commitment to the collaborative team process provides this school with abundant evidence in that category.

Ensure Student Success

The student services department at Anywhere High School includes counselors, social workers, a school psychologist, the guided study teacher, and the mentor teacher. ESSA places a heavy emphasis on high school graduation rates, so the student services department staff works to improve the school's graduation rate.

When the student services team looks at research on high school dropouts in the United States, it learns that ninth grade is the make-or-break year for high school graduation. Students who fail one or two classes are at high risk of never graduating. In fact, student grades during this year are a better predictor of who will or will not graduate from high school than race, gender, or economic status. The team also learns that students who participate in their school's extracurricular program earn better grades, have fewer absences, and are more likely to graduate than students who do not participate in school activities.

Based on this information, the school puts an intense focus on ensuring every ninth-grade student has a successful year. The program begins by bringing junior high school students into the high school on multiple occasions. The high school athletics department organizes tournaments in a variety of sports for all junior high students who will be attending Anywhere High. The department also hosts a wide range of athletic summer camps for junior high students. The art department holds two exhibitions each year that include both high school and junior high school students' work. The combined junior high and high school band and choir put on shows each year, and eighth-grade students attend the dress rehearsals of musical and dramatic productions.

> *The school puts an intense focus on ensuring every ninth-grade student has a successful year.*

Each spring, the high school invites eighth graders and their parents to attend a cocurricular fair to learn about the opportunities for freshmen to participate in athletics, intramurals, art, music, clubs, and community service. When students meet with their counselors to select their freshman courses, the counselors also ask them to name at least one cocurricular activity they might join. The counselors share this information with coaches and sponsors who follow up with a letter or personal contact to each student, encouraging him or her to join the chosen organizations.

The first day of each school year is reserved for freshmen only. They attend abbreviated sessions of all their classes; meet their teachers, advisors, and student mentors; eat lunch together; find their way around the building; and attend a pep assembly.

One of the school's key initiatives for supporting freshmen is the Freshman Advisory Program. The school assigns every new student a faculty advisor to assist with his or her transition into high school. Each advisory cohort (class) includes twenty-five students who meet four days each week. Five upper-level student mentors assist each advisor; a faculty and student committee vet each mentor. Every mentor is responsible for helping five freshmen through a successful year. The mentors explain the school's traditions and priorities, prepare their students to pass the school's Student Guidebook test, assist them in selecting an activity to join, help them organize, prepare them for other tests, and tutor them if they are having difficulty meeting proficiency standards. Mentors also are available to provide advice on such important issues as how to invite someone to the homecoming dance or study for final exams.

The student support team—comprising the school's dean, counselor, and social worker—surveys the freshmen to identify their biggest concern about entering high school. It discovers that with six different lunch periods, the freshmen's number-one fear is not having a friend to sit with at lunch. To address that concern, each mentor asks his or her five students to join the mentor for lunch the first week of school.

All the students assigned to a particular advisor also have the same guidance counselor. The counselor visits the advisory class once each week to meet with students individually and in small groups to check on how they are feeling about their high school experience, help them establish written goals of what they hope to accomplish in high school, and review their academic progress reports.

The school is very committed to timely reporting of student progress. When the faculty of Anywhere High School first began the PLC process, the school was on a nine-week grading period. Teachers were asked to send a progress report to parents of students failing at the midpoint of the nine-week period. The student support team found that fewer than 15 percent of parents receive this midterm progress report. As a result, neither parents nor members of the student support team had evidence of students' achievement levels until school had been in session for ten weeks. By then, many students were in a downward spiral in one or more courses that was difficult to reverse.

The school is very committed to timely reporting of student progress.

The student support team was asked to study more promising grading and reporting practices and then present its findings to the entire faculty, along with recommendations for addressing the concerns. The staff agreed to change its grading system from two nine-week grading periods each semester to three six-week grading periods with a mandatory progress report on every student at the midpoint of each six-week grading period. The administration agreed to provide technology that allows teachers to send twenty-five progress reports in less than ten minutes. As a result, every student, parent, advisor, and member of the student support team receives either a progress report or report card every three weeks. Students identified as struggling to learn on the progress report or report card go on a weekly checklist for monitoring their achievement.

One of the serendipitous benefits of this new procedure for monitoring students and reporting to parents is that now thousands of positive reports are going to parents, assuring them their children are doing well at Anywhere High School. Prior to the change, a progress report from the school only occurred if there was bad news about a student. Now the school is using progress reports to celebrate students as well.

Now the school is using progress reports to celebrate students as well.

Armed with this more timely information, the student support team responds when students are struggling. The standard schedule for freshmen is six classes, one study hall, an advisory period, and lunch. The study hall creates an opportunity to provide assistance to students without removing them from new direct instruction. Students in danger of failing a course are transferred from study hall to the school's tutoring center, where they get assistance from teachers and National Honor Society members.

Because all teachers are teaching the same curriculum, following the same pacing, and using the same common assessments, tutors are able to focus on specific content and skills when working with students. They are much more effective when they know a student is struggling to establish a claim in a persuasive essay as opposed to knowing the student is failing English. As soon as a student can demonstrate proficiency, he or she is transferred back to study hall.

If the student's difficulty seems due to lack of effort or failure to complete assignments, the student support team could assign the student to a program called guided study. Guided study consists of a small group of up to eight students for each period who report to the guided study teacher instead of study hall. This teacher closely monitors each student's work to ensure the student is completing his or her assignments. The guided study teacher has access to every team's website where teachers post homework assignments, so he or she can tell at a glance what each student needs to focus on during guided study periods.

This program is a radical departure from the school's traditional practice. In the past, students who were willing to fail could opt out of doing their work. Now the school is saying, "You no longer have that option. Successful people do the work. We want you to be successful. Therefore, you must complete your work, even if we need to stand over you and watch you do it."

ESSA continues to call on schools to provide evidence of improved student learning for the student body in general as well as a variety of student subgroups. Anywhere High School is well positioned to demonstrate improvement. Each teacher knows exactly what students need to learn in each unit of instruction and exactly how students will demonstrate their learning. Teachers have access to a feedback loop that allows them see how their students are performing compared to other students taking the course with a different teacher. A support system of collaborative team members helps build on strengths and address weaknesses. The school's careful monitoring of each student's learning and its comprehensive plan to provide every student with the time and support he or she needs to succeed makes sense for a school committed to high levels of student learning for *all* students.

A support system of collaborative team members helps build on strengths and address weaknesses.

Create a Positive School Climate

Many systems are in place to monitor each student's learning, but the student perspective is also important. A group of freshmen make it clear that it is impossible to be ignored if they aren't doing well academically.

One student says, "Your teacher will talk to you, your advisor will talk to you, your upperclassman mentor will start tutoring you in the subject, your counselor will come to advisory to talk to you, and your parents get notified. It's like they quadruple-team you. It's just easier to do your work and pass your classes."

The school has a systematic way of gathering information on student perceptions. The school surveys every student every year on the school climate, level of activity participation, overall satisfaction, and recommendations for improvement. For more than a decade, the school has also been gathering longitudinal survey data of a random sample of graduates one year and five years after their high school graduation.

ESSA offers schools the opportunity to provide evidence of a positive school climate and post-graduate success. This school will have no difficulty in providing that evidence.

Enrich Student Learning

ESSA allows schools to use access to rigorous curriculum as one of their indicators of quality. It seems, however, that with all this attention given to struggling students, perhaps the more capable students might be overlooked. Teachers insist, however, that this is not the case.

At one point in its history, the school provided five different ability levels in the core curriculum and placed incoming students into these levels based on a single test—the California Achievement Test (CAT). The school ranked students from highest to lowest scores on that test, and then applied a modified bell-shaped curve to the rankings. The top 10 percent of incoming students was placed in the honors program where the students have access to college-level AP courses by the time they graduate. The next 15 percent of students went to the accelerated program, which means they have a more rigorous curriculum than most students but get none of the benefits of the honors program. Fifty percent went into the regular college preparatory program. Fifteen percent went into the modified program, which had adjustments to reduce the rigor and pacing of the regular program. The bottom 10 percent of every class went into the remedial program, where the curriculum was well below grade level. Many members of the faculty vigorously defended the caps and quotas of the program. For example, the faculty was concerned that if the administration allowed an eleventh percenter into the honors program, it would erode the program's standards.

When the school adopted its new mission statement, it became evident that this placement practice was misaligned with the alleged mission. In effect, the high school was saying to junior high school teachers, "No matter how well you teach your students, we only allow 10 percent of them to access our richest curriculum, and we automatically assign 25 percent to below grade-level curriculum." The placement process was actually demotivating to both teachers and junior high school students. Placing students according to rigid caps and quotas is not a recipe for either high levels of student learning or continuous improvement.

A task force of junior high and high school teachers convened to address the issue. The task force proposed that the district establish clear standards regarding what a student leaving eighth grade should know and be able to do. It also proposed replacing the CAT with teacher-created, proficiency-based tests aligned with agreed-on standards.

The teacher task force replaces caps and quotas with benchmark targets. Any student who is able to reach the benchmark for the honors program will be admitted to the program. If 25 or 50 percent qualify, so be it. These students all have access to the honors courses. Students who meet the standard for the college-preparatory program are placed in a program that ensures they are ready to pursue college or careers after graduation.

The school collapses the five ability groups into three and reserves the lowest group for students who have not yet developed the intended knowledge and skills upon leaving high school. This third level, renamed the accelerated program, provides intensive remediation and support with double sections of English or mathematics and an hour for tutoring each day. By the time these students enter their junior year, they transition into the college-preparatory program. The remedial program under the old system of caps and quotas represented a four-year holding pen. Students never escaped it. The new program specifically accelerates learning so students can succeed in the college-preparatory curriculum by the time they are juniors.

These changes had an enormous impact on the culture of both the junior high and high school. Eighth-grade teachers became more invested in preparing their students for success at Anywhere High

School. Each junior high school department and each teacher in the core curriculum receives the results of the placement tests for their eighth graders in comparison to the results of the total group of eighth graders who took the test. This enables junior high departments and teachers to identify and address areas of strength and weakness in student performance.

One of the biggest changes at the high school is the manner in which the school responds when students are not successful. With the five-level tracking system and no process for systematic intervention in place, the standard response to a student's lack of success was to drop him or her into a lower track. If a student was not working hard enough to be successful in algebra, teachers would place him or her in pre-algebra. If the student continued to fail, they would move him or her to general mathematics.

The message students heard from the school was, "The less you do, the less you will have to do. We will keep lowering the bar for you." With fewer levels and an intervention system in place, the message became, "You need more time and support to be successful. We will give you the time and support, but we won't lower the bar."

The school has given more students greater access to a more challenging curriculum, but are students succeeding in that curriculum? In response, the school doesn't rely on impressions but, instead, is constantly monitoring evidence of the impact of its program on students.

The school doesn't rely on impressions but, instead, is constantly monitoring evidence of the impact of its program on students.

The percentage of seniors enrolling and passing at least one AP course prior to graduation has risen from 7 percent to over 90 percent. The mode score on the exams each year is 5, the highest possible score. Even though many more students are pursuing a more rigorous curriculum, the school's D and F rates have dropped from 35 percent to 4 percent. Every department is committed to entering students in academic competitions so they have opportunities to challenge themselves even further. It's fairly easy to conclude that this school will have no difficulty in demonstrating it excels in providing students with access to rigorous academic challenges.

A Reflection on Anywhere High School's Transformation

Many of the different structures put in place to support student and adult learning at Anywhere High School comply with ESSA. The administration provides adequate time for teacher collaboration as well as questions and protocols that help teams focus on the right work. They arrange student schedules so students can receive help each day without missing new direct instruction. A process provides intensive and timely monitoring of each student's learning. A system of interventions means the school has a comprehensive plan for dealing with struggling students rather than relying on each teacher to solve the problem.

> *A system of interventions means the school has a comprehensive plan for dealing with struggling students rather than relying on each teacher to solve the problem.*

With the new flexibility afforded states under ESSA, it would be wonderful to see states support districts in replicating these structures and processes in their schools. They are necessary to support improved student learning, but they are not sufficient. Anywhere High School's success is a function of the mindset, expectations, and commitments of the people within the school. States cannot mandate mindsets, but they can provide the tools to help educators become more reflective about their practice. They can provide templates to help educators gather evidence on the current reality of their schools, a synthesis of research on best practices in school improvement, prioritized standards, high-quality assessment items, protocols for analyzing student work, examples of high-quality student work at different grade levels, video libraries of effective instructional practices, success stories of schools showing dramatic improvement, and a support team to work with struggling schools to identify and solve problems. (Visit **go.SolutionTree.com /PLCbooks** for the free reproducible "A Data Picture of Our School," which offers a template teachers can use to record this kind of data.)

> *States cannot mandate mindsets, but they can provide the tools to help educators become more reflective about their practice.*

In the final analysis, states must develop a new mindset for school improvement if they hope to support new expectations among educators. If more schools are going to operate like Anywhere High School, states must move away from the sanction-driven, evaluative approach of the past and embrace a responsibility to promote capacity-building strategies to improve their schools.

The Right Work Remains the Same

Although the school in this chapter is a high school, we want to emphasize that we could use an example of an elementary school or a middle school just as easily because *the right work of a PLC remains the right work across grade levels*. So far, we have emphasized the following core foundation elements.

- Collaborative teams of educators replace individual classrooms as the fundamental structure of the school. Team members take collective responsibility for student learning, work interdependently, and hold each other mutually accountable for achieving SMART goals that continuously improve student learning.

- Teams provide students with access to a guaranteed and viable curriculum, unit by unit.

- Teams monitor student learning on an ongoing basis in their classrooms each day and through at least one team-developed common formative assessment for each unit of instruction.

- Teams use the results from their common formative assessments to identify the following.

  - Students who need additional time and support to demonstrate proficiency on each skill or concept of the unit

  - Students who are highly proficient and need extension or acceleration to advance their learning

  - Individual team members whose results indicate they have strengths to share with colleagues or weaknesses members could help address

  - Areas in which no team member is able to help students achieve the intended unit outcomes, and training the team members might strengthen their instructional strategies in those areas (Visit **go.SolutionTree.com/PLCbooks** for the free reproducible "Data Analysis Protocol.")

- The school creates a system of interventions that guarantees all struggling students receive additional time and support for learning, regardless of their teachers. This time and support occurs during the school day and does not remove students from new direct instruction.

All of these elements and the assumptions and mindset that support them are evident in a PLC, regardless of which grade levels constitute a school. There may, however, be structural differences in how an elementary school as opposed to how a secondary school—middle, junior high, and high—implements these elements.

For example, whereas secondary school teams are more likely to be course specific (for example, all biology teachers, all seventh-grade mathematics teachers, or all ninth-grade English teachers), teams in elementary schools are more likely to be grade-level specific (all third-grade teachers or all kindergarten teachers). Because elementary schools are likely to have a single specialist teacher in subject areas such as art, music, and physical education, these teachers are more likely to be members of job-alike district teams that rely more heavily on technology to support their team meetings. Whereas high schools are more likely to have several school counselors or special education teachers who can form a team with their peers, elementary schools may assign counselors and special education teachers to a particular grade-level team based on perceived needs.

Structures for intervention may look different in a secondary school versus an elementary school. For example, secondary schools may provide one or more locations or centers for intervention to take place, and students report to those centers at designated times to receive help. Elementary schools are more likely to designate a specific intervention time for each team during the school day in which additional staff members push into the grade-level classrooms to provide more concentrated assistance.

Educators in elementary schools are typically more able to use parents as partners in their children's education. In many high-performing elementary PLCs, grade-level teams create common calendars to alert parents to the skills and concepts taught at particular times. The teams provide study materials for parents to help them review those skills and concepts with their children at home. The teams also provide feedback sheets that allow parents to advise the teacher whether their child is demonstrating proficiency at home or is in need of additional time and support at school.

Secondary school teachers are less likely to ask parents to assist with tutoring students in algebra, chemistry, or French, but many teachers can provide parents with suggestions for discussing topics from the classroom with their children at home. However, both elementary and secondary school teachers should have a process for gathering relevant information about a student from the parent's perspective. A teacher may be an expert in third-grade curriculum, how to create an engaging biology lab, or the difficult transitions students undergo in middle school, but parents are the experts when it comes to their own children. High-performing PLCs strive for two-way communication at all grade levels, allowing teachers and parents to share their respective expertise.

Just as the needs of students vary at different grade levels, the structures within the school to address those needs may vary as well. However, all PLCs establish a firm foundation of shared purpose, a clear vision of what the school must become to fulfill that purpose, the collective commitments necessary to move the school toward its vision, and SMART goals to determine benchmarks of progress. The following three big ideas that drive the process are always evident and the four critical questions (see pages 55–56) that guide the work of teams remain the same, regardless of the grade levels assigned to a particular school:

Just as the needs of students vary at different grade levels, the structures within the school to address those needs may vary as well.

A Focus on Learning. The first (and the biggest) of the big ideas is based on the premise that *the fundamental purpose of the school is to ensure that all students learn at high levels (grade level or higher)*. This focus on and commitment to the learning of each student are the very essence of a *learning community*. . . .

A Collaborative Culture and Collective Responsibility. The second big idea driving the PLC process is that in order to help ensure all students learn at high levels, *educators must work collaboratively and take collective responsibility for the success of each student.* Working collaboratively is not optional, but instead is an expectation and requirement of employment. . . .

A Results Orientation. The third big idea that drives the work of PLCs is the need for a *results orientation.* To assess their effectiveness in helping all students learn, educators in a PLC focus on results—evidence of student learning. They then use that evidence of learning to inform and improve their professional practice and respond to individual students who need intervention or enrichment. (DuFour et al., 2016, pp. 11–12)

Some educators contend that they can't focus on implementing the PLC process because they are preoccupied with meeting federal mandates, such as NCLB or RTTT. This assertion is highly questionable since nothing in those laws or regulations forbids educators from implementing any element of the PLC process. U.S. Senator Lamar Alexander, one of the chief architects of ESSA, has further undercut that argument by telling state legislatures that they should operate under the assumption that ESSA allows them to do whatever they like to improve their schools (Ujifusa, 2016).

Sometimes educators tell us their schools are too small or too large to be a PLC. They are too urban, too rural, or too suburban. Their students are too needy to benefit from the process or they are such high performers there is no need to seek improvement. These educators prefer to ignore the examples that refute all these claims.

A school committed to the status quo always finds a reason not to pursue more promising practices. We contend that when a professional *knows* better, he or she has an obligation to *do* better. Our professionals know better. We can create better conditions for learning for both students and adults. We know what those conditions are. What is required is the

> *We contend that when a professional knows better, he or she has an obligation to do better.*

resolve to bring about that transformation. No legislation can provide educators with that resolve. Education professionals must find it within themselves because they recognize the moral imperative of helping *all* students learn at high levels.

In the next chapter, we examine how leaders at the district level can use ESSA to support deep implementation of continuous improvement processes in their schools.

CHAPTER 5

A View From
the District

E SSA offers states and local school districts a striking alternative to the innovation incentives and sanctions that prevailed from 2001 to 2016. After presenting a brief review of federal-level innovation strategies, we consider how districts can fundamentally redefine education accountability in innovative ways. These innovations, taken as a whole, create a laboratory for identifying the most (and least) promising education interventions and leadership strategies using a variety of quantitative and qualitative analyses. There are three fundamental requirements of ESSA with regard to state, district, and school accountability (Association for Supervision and Curriculum Development, 2015):

> ESSA requires states to give "much greater weight" to academic indicators than to other indicators. . . .
>
> ESSA requires states to use additional (nonacademic) measures "that allows for meaningful differentiation" among schools. . . .
>
> ESSA requires states to help districts improve conditions for learning. (pp. 4–5)

Implementing regulations for the law may provide greater definition for phrases like *greater weight* and *meaningful differentiation*, but it is also possible that, in the aftermath of the definitional quagmires of phrases like *highly qualified teachers* from previous legislation, the U.S. Department of Education may defer to the states in these matters. However ambiguous or specific future implementing regulations may be, there are some certainties in the law to which districts can immediately respond. Each school district in the country has the requirement—and, we would add, the *opportunity*—to create support and improvement strategies, particularly in low-performing schools.

This will undoubtedly lead to striking differences among districts, and that is as it should be. Rural, suburban, and urban systems have different needs and require different levels of measurement. In small systems with only a single third-grade classroom, the variation in performance of one or two students can make the difference between a school branded as failing and one branded as succeeding. In large systems, a high average score can mask the needs of students who deserve support and intervention.

The most important ESSA accountability provisions explicitly require a shift from an almost total reliance on test scores to a combination of student achievement measures and indicators that reflect teaching, leadership, culture, climate, and what has been broadly described as *conditions for learning.*

According to the U.S. Department of Education (2016), states must have a combination of test data and learning environment information that leads to student performance. Superficially, the department says:

> States have increased flexibility to take a more holistic view of school performance based on multiple measures, including achievement in reading and math, academic progress in elementary and middle schools, graduate rates in high school, rates of progress for English learners achieving language proficiency, and a state-determined indicator of school quality of student success.

The key to this increased flexibility is that state and district measures must be evidence based.

The key to this increased flexibility is that state and district measures must be *evidence based*—that is, each accountability indicator expresses a hypothesis about the relationship between that indicator and desired student results, and those hypotheses must be tested against the evidence of student achievement.

An important part of any inquiry process is not the magical thinking that assumes every hypothesis is valid, but rather the real world in which some hypotheses are confirmed and others are not. Therefore, the creation of an indicator for the influences of teaching, leadership, and other factors on student achievement may lead to a strong association, a weak or no association, or even a negative association. Although the recognition of failed hypotheses may be new in federal policymaking, it is certainly not new to education leaders.

Research from more than two thousand school-improvement plans and achievement data from more than one million students reveals that of the twenty-one state- and provincial-mandated elements, only a handful stood out as strongly related to gains in student achievement (Reeves, 2011). Three of the most powerful variables in that study—(1) focus, (2) prioritization, and (3) monitoring—directly contradict the frequent mandates that require more initiatives and less focus. And each additional priority diminishes the ability of local school leaders to monitor progress.

How Test-Based Accountability Undermines Innovation

Since 2001, an external authority dictates the results of test-based accountability, while allowing states to innovate with regard to the *how* of teaching, learning, and leadership. But after eight years of NCLB and another eight years of RTTT, the United States ranks below average in education innovations, according to the OECD (2014a). The United States ranks behind traditional education systems, such as Singapore and Hong Kong, and also behind countries and territories within Turkey, Italy, and Slovenia, to name a few. There were some bright spots—a 31 percent increase among U.S. teachers who ask students to observe and describe natural phenomena; a 27 percent gain in individualized reading instruction in primary school classrooms; and a 17 percent gain in mathematics instructions that require students to elaborate on their answers. Not surprisingly, the greatest gain in innovation is the use of assessments for monitoring progress, as more than 97 percent of U.S. secondary school students are enrolled in schools using this practice. Nevertheless, in the OECD (2014a) overall composite innovation index from 2000 to 2011, the United States remains a laggard in education innovation.

With the benefit of hindsight, it is tempting to blame federal-level micromanagement for the failure of innovative thinking.

With the benefit of hindsight, it is tempting to blame federal-level micromanagement for the failure of innovative thinking. However, since 2001, the U.S. Department of Education funded tens of billions of dollars in innovation grants targeted specifically for school improvement, teacher preparation, technology, and other areas deemed to be innovative (U.S. Department of Education, 2017), with little to show for it.

Some of greatest investments are assessments based either on the Common Core State Standards or on individual state standards, but schools are quickly abandoning those assessments (Jochim & McGuinn, 2016). Although the Common Core was initially adopted by forty-five states with the intent to use its student assessments, as of the spring of 2016, only twenty-one states were still using them (Gewertz, 2016). The point is not to debate the advantages or disadvantages of a particular assessment scheme, but rather to note the evidence that neither punishments nor rewards from the federal government succeed in establishing or maintaining even the most basic education innovations.

In chapter 4, we suggest three levels of an effective accountability system under ESSA. The following section details what this system looks like.

Accountability as a Learning System

The three levels of this accountability system include (1) state-mandated measures, (2) school and district indicators, and (3) how education leaders put all the data together to draw cause-and-effect links in student achievement.

Level 1 focuses on state-mandated accountability measures. In addition to those federal law measures, many states may want to add level 1 indicators that address student safety (for example, freedom from violence and access to clean water, food, and air), equity (access to a rigorous curriculum and effective teaching), learning-focused collaboration in schools that function as PLCs, and other essential values that each state believes is important for its schools.

Schools and districts develop level 2 indicators, which focus on the actions of teachers, leaders, and local policymakers. These factors influence the learning environment addressed by ESSA, and it is the link between level 2 (causes) and level 1 (effects) that creates a learning system. Level 3 of new accountability systems represents the distinction between accountability as a mere bureaucratic requirement and accountability as a learning system. Let's consider an example of all three levels of accountability at work.

There are fundamental accountability indicators on which nearly every stakeholder agrees. These level 1 indicators have broad application. They address common questions such as the following.

- Are students safe?

- Are students coming to school more than 95 percent of the time?

- Are students proficient at their grade level in reading and mathematics?

- Are students finishing high school?

- Are students leaving high school prepared for college or work?

Unfortunately, this is where most accountability indicators stop. Level 1 indicators are necessary but insufficient. What stakeholders and policymakers need is a holistic system that includes not only effects (level 1) but causes (level 2).

Every U.S. school is required to assess student success in reading comprehension, and each state must create methods of assessing this vital skill. Those results are level 1 indicators. But what teaching and leadership strategies are most effective in improving reading comprehension in a very diverse set of schools? Will the strategies for schools serving a largely poverty-stricken student population who does not speak English at home be the same as those in schools in which most students come to kindergarten reading fluently? Will the allocation of time and resources for literacy instruction be the same for students who need one year of gains in learning to show progress as those for middle school students who are reading at a second-grade level?

ESSA offers an opportunity to provide thoughtful responses to these questions in a way that not only meets the unique needs of each school and district but also creates a body of evidence to inform education decision making across the United States.

Level 2 indicators for literacy that schools and districts might choose include the following.

- Time for literacy instruction

- Percentage of literacy instruction includes rich teacher talk, storybook reading, phonological awareness activities, alphabet activities, support for emergent reading and writing, shared book experiences, and integrated content-focused activities (Roskos, Christie, & Richgels, 2003)

    We recognize that there are divergent views on the quantity and descriptions of reading instruction essentials, but in a learning system, each school must express a hypothesis about what effective reading instruction is, monitor the degree to which that instruction takes place, and then measure the relationship between instruction and student learning.

- Number of student writing requirements (outside English language arts instruction) as clear evidence of the link between student writing and improved reading comprehension (National Writing Project, 2010)

Similarly, schools and districts can hypothesize the link between mathematics instruction and student learning. Examples of level 2 indicators for mathematics might include the following.

- Percentage of student mathematics journal entries that receive a rating of proficient or higher on collaboratively scored units

- A classroom structure that supports students working together in small groups each day rather than relying solely on large-group instruction

- Number of mathematics assessments (outside direct mathematics instruction)

There are many opportunities in science, social studies, physical education, music, and art for students to reinforce essential mathematics knowledge and skills. These sorts of indicators allow the entire faculty to support the more visible mathematics accountability indicators.

Level 2 indicators also can include measurements of student engagement, such as the following.

- Percentage of students engaged in two or more extra-curricular activities

  Douglas (Reeves, 2009) cites a study that reveals a strong association between extracurricular involvement and student achievement, with the greatest gains in performance when students increase their level of involvement from zero to two activities. This trend continues through involvement in four activities, but then levels out. It may be tempting for faculty advisors to recruit the same actively engaged students they already know—the two-sport athlete becomes a four-sport athlete, and the students involved in government also lead the French Club, Odyssey of the Mind, and Chess Club. But the evidence suggests that the greatest impact on the school's academic climate comes from recruiting disengaged students or those only minimally engaged in a single activity (Reeves, 2009).

- Percentage of students occupying leadership positions, creating an incentive for broad-based alternatives and rotating leadership responsibilities

Although research suggests that these example accountability indicators show promise, they are not necessarily effective in every context (Reeves, 2004). We present accountability indicators as hypotheses to be tested, not as mandates for districts to follow. With each passing year, changes in student needs and district goals suggest new and better level 2 indicators. At the end of each year, careful analysis will suggest the relationship, if any, between level 2 (cause) and level 1 (effect) indicators. Appendix A, "Sample School-Level Accountability Indicators" (page 117), offers an extensive list of sample level 2 accountability indicators.

Cause-and-Effect Links in Student Achievement

Level 3 in new accountability systems is how education leaders put all the data together to draw inferences about the relationship between the school's teaching and leadership variables and student achievement indicators. There are at least four possible relationships between cause-and-effect indicators in their accountability system for schools and districts to consider. These include (1) positive, (2) little or no, (3) negative, or (4) nonlinear.

Positive Relationships

Figure 5.1 illustrates the positive relationships possibility. The horizontal axis displays frequency of student writing, and the vertical axis displays student proficiency in reading comprehension.

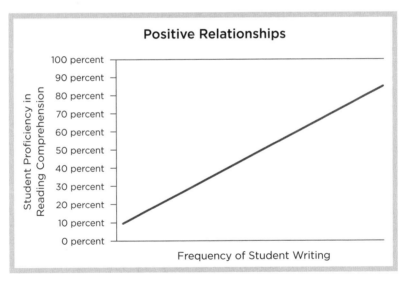

Figure 5.1: Positive relationships.

Little or No Relationships

In this situation, the degree of a school-improvement plan's conformity with external format requirements may have little or no relationship to student proficiency. As figure 5.2 suggests, schools with both

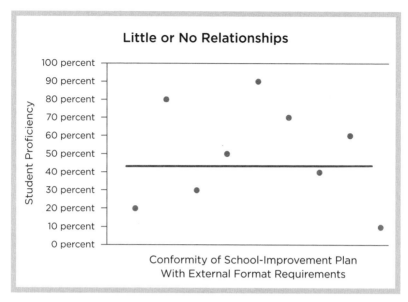

Figure 5.2: Little or no relationships.

high and low conformity with plan design requirements have both high and low achievement. This doesn't suggest that the plans are bad, but rather that those requiring and monitoring school plans might reconsider the hypothesis that the energy school leaders invest in planning documents leads to higher achievement.

Negative Relationships

When it comes to the number of initiatives and student results, we find negative relationships. As Fullan (2011a) notes, schools "have not been able to focus on strategic actions that would mobilize scores of people at the school, district, state, and federal levels" (p. viii) in large measure because "we have had punctuated decades of dramatic and urgent calls for system reform coupled with equally dramatic failures" (p. vii). This failure of focus or the growing number of instructional and leadership initiatives has been strongly associated with negative student performance, as figure 5.3 (page 80) illustrates.

When it comes to the number of initiatives and student results, we find negative relationships.

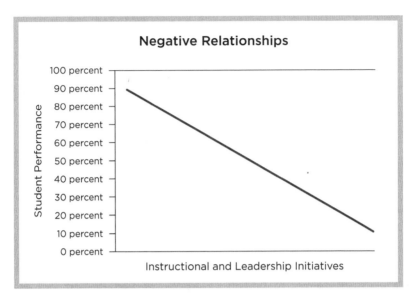

Figure 5.3: Negative relationships.

Nonlinear Relationships

Whereas straight lines and linear correlation coefficients measured mathematically illustrate the first three relationships, much in life, particularly in education leadership, is nonlinear. For example, at first many instructional initiatives have little relationship to student achievement in large part because implementation is haphazard and incomplete. If you assume the relationships between causes and effects are linear, you might jump to the conclusion that a particular teaching or leadership strategy has no impact (see figure 5.2, page 79) or even a negative impact (see figure 5.3).

Effective implementation of teaching and leadership strategies requires time, professional learning, feedback, and deliberate practice.

However, our observation is that effective implementation of teaching and leadership strategies requires time, professional learning, feedback, and deliberate practice. Thus, if there are four levels of implementation, as on the horizontal axis of figure 5.4, only the highest level of implementation is related to student achievement. That is why even exceptionally powerful ideas, such as the PLC at Work process, described in the

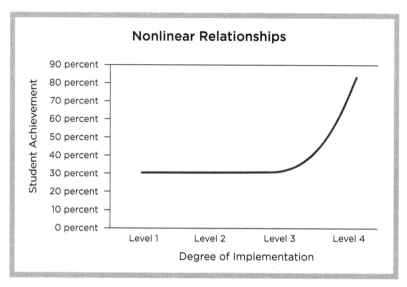

Figure 5.4: Nonlinear relationships.

introduction, as well as in the story of Anywhere High School, can lead to enormous frustration when schools only implement improvement processes in a superficial way.

As important as teaching and leadership strategies are as cause variables in a new accountability system, there remains an essential area in the work of school districts completely overlooked in previous accountability systems—the work of central office administrators. We now turn our attention to this subject.

District Central Office Accountability Indicators

The district administration stereotype is that it is far removed from the realities of the classroom and more concerned with bureaucratic compliance than making real teaching, learning, and leadership improvements. Nevertheless, ESSA requirements to assess the learning environment offer district administrators the opportunity to identify and document actions at the district level that are most—and least—related to student achievement. In the case of many central office departments (for example, finance, facilities, food service, transportation, technology, and human resources), we typically notice their performance only when things go wrong. But effective accountability indicators consider the impact that these departments and others make in improving the learning environment.

Effective accountability indicators consider the impact that these departments and others make in improving the learning environment.

Effective financial managers not only balance the books but also save money through effective contract management that they can reallocate for instructional needs. Facilities managers play a direct role in providing students a safe and secure environment as well as identifying and avoiding disruptions, such as asbestos contamination that can cause enormous upheavals in schools.

By attending to building safety in all facilities—from those for instruction to those for storage, maintenance, and administration—facilities managers can avoid the human and financial costs associated with workplace accidents.

Food service managers play a role in determining whether a student is alert and interested in the afternoon or stuffed and lethargic after an unhealthy lunch. Transportation managers ensure that students arrive at school safely and on time. Moreover, bus drivers who have positive relationships with students can minimize time for discipline and student disruptions.

Technology managers can, with great customer service, dramatically increase classroom time for instruction and reduce the amount of time for setting up devices. Human resources managers can ensure that the district instructional leaders have a full pipeline of qualified teachers and other staff members and, with careful selection and interviewing processes, reduce the costs of turnover.

Appendix B, "Sample System-Level Accountability Indicators" (page 129), lists some specific indicators that districts might consider, each of which highlights the performance of central office departments. One of the clear lessons of traditional accountability systems is that what does not get measured remains unnoticed. Thus, essential school elements ranging from preK to calculus, from music to libraries, from health and safety to technology, all appear as priorities in name only; traditional accountability measures ignore them. With accountability as a learning system, schools can restore their priorities to high levels of public visibility and make direct connections to student learning.

The Value of Qualitative Insights

While it is helpful to draw inferences on the quantitative relationship between teaching and leadership variables and student achievement variables, one of the most enduring lessons of education research is that you can't measure everything with a number. Some of the most important insights from great scholars in education, including Howard Gardner (2007); Andy Hargreaves, Alan Boyle, and Alma Harris (2014); and Michael Fullan (2011a), are the result of keen observation, deep case studies, and nonquantitative inferences.

> *One of the most enduring lessons of education research is that you can't measure everything with a number.*

While data analysis informs these influential researchers, they are not subservient to it. Moreover, there is no neat mathematical formula to easily observe large trends from different perspectives, as Gardner (2000) did with art, science, and music; and as Hargreaves and Fullan (2012) did with education, sports, and business. The absence of statistics in their studies does not render their work any less rigorous but rather offers a different perspective that informs leadership judgments about education.

Similarly, the ESSA requirement that accountability measures offer meaningful differences among schools should not solely depend on traditional measures of statistical significance. Use of the term *significance* in education statistics most often means only that the differences between two groups of students are unlikely to be the result of random variation. Moreover, statistical significance is largely a function of differences between groups as well as the size of the student population.

Thus, there can be very meaningful differences between two classrooms or two schools, differences that have practical applications for teachers and school leaders, but are not necessarily significant statistically because the number of students is small. The built-in flexibility of ESSA allows for a variety of measures, and district accountability systems most likely to lead to system-level learning depend on numbers as well as deep reflection, systematic observation, and qualitative study.

In the next chapter, we shift our focus from the school and district levels to the state. We examine the roles that key stakeholders can play in the application of accountability systems under ESSA.

CHAPTER 6

How States Can Transform Opportunity Into Action

In chapter 3, we identify what states *must do*—and what they *must stop doing*—in order to have a more positive impact on student achievement and teaching effectiveness. Certainly, federal micromanagement from 2001–2016 demonstrates the ineffectiveness of that approach. However, this does not imply that states are mere distributors of federal grants. Rather, states play an essential role in creating boundaries in which school districts must operate. While there are certainly variations in the needs of rural, suburban, and urban schools, there is no variation in the essential values and principles that guide school improvement.

Although *how* collaborative teams are structured may vary significantly, collaboration on the right work remains an imperative that applies to every education system, from the smallest K–12 district in a single building to the largest and most complex urban systems. Moreover, the four critical questions for every team remain constant (DuFour et al., 2016):

> *Although* how *collaborative teams are structured may vary significantly, collaboration on the right work remains an imperative that applies to every education system.*

1. What knowledge, skills, and dispositions should every student acquire as a result of this unit, this course, or this grade level?

2. How will we know when each student has acquired the essential knowledge and skills?

3. How will we respond when some students do not learn?

4. How can we extend the learning for students who are already proficient?

This focus on learning, assessment, intervention, and extension represents the discretionary boundaries of the school or district. In this chapter, we consider a three-level accountability system framework for how states can encourage innovation at the local level while maintaining the essential boundaries of effective professional learning. It also offers a vision of how to transform the promise of ESSA into an engine of education innovation by considering the lessons learned; using menus, not mandates; providing a framework for state innovation; and focusing on state accountability as a learning system.

Lessons Learned

As we stress in chapter 1, you must view the general enthusiasm about ESSA opportunities for states through a historical lens. Just as the bipartisan euphoria over NCLB soon deteriorated into universal disappointment, the Obama administration's "yes, we can" enthusiasm seemed to erode into "now, you must" practices that alienated the very educators called on to improve our schools. Excitement for state discretionary decision making may become tomorrow's unpopular mandate. Thus, leaders at every level should make policy as if they are testing hypotheses. In other words, each state-level education policy should represent the expression of an "If . . . then" statement.

Leaders at every level should make policy as if they are testing hypotheses.

Following are some inferences we drew from the punitive policies adopted in the wake of NCLB, starting in 2001, and the incentives of RTTT, starting in 2009.

- "If we threaten and intimidate teachers and administrators with mandatory terminations, reorganizations, and redistribution of staff members, then student achievement will improve."

- "If we publicly humiliate school leaders, policymakers, and teachers with grades associated with each school, then student achievement will improve."

- "If we publish the results of teacher effectiveness ratings based on, among other things, gains in student test scores, then teaching practices and student achievement will improve."

The list of education policies with greater enthusiasm than evidence is a long one (DuFour, 2015). However, despite this checkered history, education systems at the state and district levels have expressed newly proposed policies as hypotheses. Policymakers research, advocate, and implement—rarely asking if reality conforms to expectations. NCLB uses the terms *scientifically based* and *research based* more than 250 times and provides generous funding for the What Works Clearing-house. The What Works Clearinghouse (https://ies.ed.gov/ncee/wwc) is a publicly available resource coordinated by the National Center for Educational Evaluation and Regional Support (NCEE), whose intent is to help education decision makers identify which studies are most rigorous. The criteria include factors such as random assignment and the absence of confounding variables that might influence results.

We view this project with grave reservations for two reasons. First, it is unlikely and possibly inappropriate to randomly assign students away from a promising teaching practice in order to serve as a control group in the name of better research. More important, we consider it preposterous that any study of real students could lack confounding variables (such as different families, languages, home environments, nutrition, and so on). The difference between studies that do not have confounding variables and those that do is not a difference in rigor, but a difference in how forthcoming the researchers are.

A more precise label might be the What *Worked* Clearinghouse, because research inevitably looks in the rearview mirror, taking into account local conditions and challenges, rather than a clear-eyed view to the road ahead.

Because the discretion ESSA gives to state policymakers might not be permanent, now is a good opportunity to engage in a hypothesis-testing approach to state policymaking. This entails not only seizing opportunities for innovation but also establishing an analysis discipline that is more likely to allow sustainable effective policies even as the political winds of the future shift.

While many hail ESSA as a striking return of state power over federal education policy, Alia Wong (2015) of *The Atlantic* warns that "for all the breathless hype, the [ESSA] legislation seems unlikely to produce many changes that are actually visible on the ground."

This chapter addresses the immediate, practical, and sustainable actions that state education leaders can take over the years ahead.

Menus, Not Mandates

The phrase that best encapsulates the shift from NCLB to ESSA is *menus, not mandates.* In the view of the National Education Association (NEA; Álvarez, 2016), "It's one thing to be invited to dinner, where— maybe—you're asked to bring an appetizer or dessert. It's a game-changer when you're the one deciding the main course, requesting the side dishes, and setting the table."

One item missing from the NEA's analogy is that educators are also the ones who clean up after the dinner party, no matter how civilized or rowdy the diners. The power of public input for ESSA is enormous, and as previous education legislation demonstrates, it is not merely the words of the law itself, but the implementing regulations that determine the degree to which the legislation's promises are realized. For example, section 1111(b)(1)(G) of ESSA makes it clear that states have wide discretion on matters of standards and assessments:

(G) PROHIBITIONS.—

(i) STANDARDS REVIEW OR APPROVAL.—A State shall not be required to submit any standards developed under this subsection to the Secretary for review or approval.

(ii) FEDERAL CONTROL.—The Secretary shall not have the authority to mandate, direct, control, coerce, or exercise any direction or supervision over any of the challenging State academic standards adopted or implemented by a State. (ESSA, 2015)

Although the federal role appears to be limited in general, since 2001, the U.S. Department of Education can wield extensive power with or without federal legislation (Reeves, 2001). A combination of funding prerogatives and rulemaking continue to make the federal government an influential part of public education.

> *A combination of funding prerogatives and rulemaking continue to make the federal government an influential part of public education.*

In contrast to the limits of federal authority, ESSA grants broad discretion to state education leaders to make and enforce policies. The most extensive policymaker requirements are broadly inclusive rulemaking processes. In general, however, the shift of ESSA to local control is a shift to the states, not to schools and districts. Following are some ways to help the implementation of ESSA go more smoothly.

Include Educators, Administrators, and the Public in the Process

Participants from a wide variety of stakeholder groups must develop a library of federal rules as part of ESSA implementation. Some of these groups include parents and teachers from traditional public schools and charter schools, career and technical educators, principals and other school leaders, local school board members, private school representatives, specialized instructional support personnel and paraprofessionals, public chartering agencies representatives, and charter school leaders, to name a few. Remarkably, the law's public comment periods range from fifteen to sixty days, so the most organized, connected, and watchful organizations have the greatest impact on making rules.

Use Menus to Bring Stakeholders Together

The use of menus rather than mandates allows state education policymakers to consider a variety of points of view and, rather than finding the one true path to education reform—a path littered with frustration and failure—states have the opportunity to encourage variation of practice within the boundaries

> *States have the opportunity to encourage variation of practice within the boundaries of values, principles, and science.*

of values, principles, and science. To be clear: the menu may include many different methods of teacher collaboration within and among schools and districts, but the absence of collaboration is off the menu.

Assessments, interventions, and extension methods vary among schools and districts, but based on our observations of and work with thousands of schools and hundreds of districts, it is contrary to education principles and the consensus of education research for a school or district to fail to address the four critical questions of learning from the PLC at Work framework:

1. What knowledge, skills, and dispositions should every student acquire as a result of this unit, this course, or this grade level?

2. How will we know when each student has acquired the essential knowledge and skills?

3. How will we respond when some students do not learn?

4. How can we extend the learning for students who are already proficient?

Not all these alternatives will be fruitful, but every science teacher knows that people learn more from error than from uncertainty. It is the continuous process of trying, testing, evaluating, and improving that leads to gains in every field of endeavor, including teaching and education leadership. A process of menus—even when some menu choices turn out to be unpalatable—is more effective and sustainable than a list of mandates.

A Framework for State Innovation in Education

Some critics warn that ESSA merely replaces an intransigent bureaucracy in Washington, DC, with equally difficult bureaucracies in state capitals. It does not have to be this way. States can use ESSA flexibility to provide simultaneous loose and tight controls that safeguard, or keep tight, the most fundamental values and practices for students, while allowing for a variety of ways to achieve these objectives through a flexible, or loose, approach with teachers (DuFour et al., 2016).

Specifically, states can use a three-level accountability model that honors essential mandates for what we might call *safety and value issues* while largely deferring how to achieve the overall objectives to districts and individual schools. We outline a three-level accountability model as a learning system, including state-mandated accountability and school- and district-based accountability, and then putting it all together to determine whether to continue, abandon, modify, or implement education practices to meet these goals.

Educational accountability policies can take one of two paths—(1) accountability as a system of penalties and rewards or (2) accountability as a learning system. If the goal of accountability is simply to provide rewards and punishments, then the U.S. Department of Education and the state departments of education just need to study test data, shaming those schools, districts, and states with low scores and praising those with high scores. The problem with this approach is that it does not help education policymakers and leaders to improve the performance of students, teachers, and leaders. ESSA offers state and local education leaders a better path—accountability as a learning system.

Student achievement on formative and summative assessments forms only one piece of the accountability puzzle. In order to transform accountability policies into a learning system, schools must consider not only test scores but also the actions of teachers and leaders. With an understanding of how the actions of teachers and leaders influence student achievement, accountability systems can do more than offer the facile advice to raise test scores. We can do better, providing insights about the professional practices that will lead to improved student achievement.

Level 1 comprises systemwide indicators, representing the priorities common to all schools. These indicators might include safety, attendance, and various measures of academic achievement and growth. Level 2 indicators represent the causes—measurable indicators in teaching, leadership, parental involvement, community support, and so on. These indicators vary from each school, though policymakers at the state level may wish to create a menu from which schools select the indicators that are most appropriate for them. Level 3 is a narrative, including qualitative descriptions of the school environment and an explanation of how the cause-and-effect variables fit—or don't fit—together.

Level 1: State-Mandated Accountability

Level 1 in our accountability model includes matters common to every district and every school—whether urban or rural, large or small, economically disadvantaged or wealthy, or full of English-speaking students or newcomers to the United States. Considering the diversity of school needs, the number of mandatory safety and value issues is relatively small. Examples of level 1 indicators that apply to every school include quantitative indicators such as attendance, student and staff safety, and a measure of academic student achievement.

Although ESSA requires reading and mathematics testing in grades 3–8 and an additional high school performance assessment, states may also include other essentials from early childhood education through secondary school performance. States also must establish ground rules for effective collaboration, replacing the encyclopedic lists of teacher and administrator compliance indicators with a solid framework that includes collaboration, common assessment, effective intervention, and enrichment. Thus, the state establishes boundaries within which local innovation occurs.

This represents a fundamental shift away from test-based accountability that considers only *effects* without identifying the underlying *causes* of student achievement. Thus, if we only consider student effect variables, we are like those who exhort overweight teenagers to shed some pounds but fail to consider whether weight loss is due to a thoughtful combination of diet and exercise or a disastrous combination of eating disorders and drug abuse. Weight loss alone—the effect variable—would never tell the whole story any more than test scores alone distinguish between genuine improvements in academic performance or other variables, such as shifts in student populations, modifications to test format and composition, or even cheating. Level 1 is a necessary but insufficient formula for education accountability. The second level of accountability—school- and district-based indicators of teaching, learning, and leadership—flings open the door of innovation, making accountability a learning system.

Level 2: School- and District-Based Accountability

Although we dedicate our professional lives to the advocacy and application of research-based solutions in schools, the inevitable question from skeptics is, "How do we know it will work here, in our schools, with our students?" It's a fair question, and "trust us" is rarely a satisfactory response.

A better option is for state departments to provide a menu of research-based solutions. Schools then choose some—not more than half a dozen—for implementation. Each choice is a hypothesis: "If we fully implement this intervention, then student achievement (or behavior, attendance, health, engagement, and so on) will improve." For example, the use of frequent common formative assessments at every grade level and in every subject is at the heart of effective teacher collaboration because it orients all teaching toward a common objective. While the content, format, and frequency of common formative assessments may vary (school and district discretion at level 2), the existence of common formative assessments is constant (state boundaries in level 1).

> *A better option is for state departments to provide a menu of research-based solutions.*

It is imperative that the state menu items are sufficiently broad in scope to meet the needs of a wide variety of schools within the state, but that they do not pretend to meet the needs of every school. In addition, it is vital that these menu items are not binary choices—"We adopted the program" or "We did not adopt the program"—but rather, parts on an implementation continuum. For example, not every school and district that claims to be a PLC can cite evidence of improved student learning.

In order for accountability to be a learning system, the system must assess not merely the adoption of a program but also *the degree of implementation on a continuum for each unit of analysis, whether that is a district, school, grade level, or department.* Figure 6.1 (pages 94–95) provides an example of such a continuum. While it would be difficult to find a single educator or administrator who has not been exposed to one type of data-driven decision-making training or another, there

DIRECTIONS: Individually, silently, and *honestly* assess the current reality of your school's implementation of each indicator listed in the left column. Consider what evidence or anecdotes support your assessment. This form may also be used to assess district or team implementation.

Individuals, teams, and schools seek relevant data and information and use them to promote continuous improvement.

Indicator	Pre-Initiating	Initiating	Implementing	Developing	Sustaining
Collaborative teams of teachers regard ongoing analysis of evidence of student learning as a critical element in the teaching and learning process. Teachers receive frequent and timely information regarding student achievement. They use that information to: • Respond to students who are experiencing difficulty • Enrich and extend the learning of students who are proficient • Inform and improve the individual and collective practice of members • Identify team professional development needs • Measure progress toward team goals	The only process for monitoring student learning is the individual classroom teacher and annual state, provincial, or national assessments. Assessment results are used primarily to report on student progress rather than to improve professional practice. Teachers fall into a predictable pattern: they teach, test, hope for the best, and then move on to the next unit.	The district has created benchmark assessments that are administered several times throughout the year. There is often considerable lag time before teachers receive the results. Most teachers pay little attention to the results. They regard the assessment as perhaps beneficial to the district but of little use to them. Principals are encouraged to review the results of state assessments with staff, but the fact that the results aren't available until months after the assessment and the lack of specificity mean they are of little use in helping teachers improve their practice.	Teams have been asked to create and administer common formative assessments and to analyze the results together. Many teachers are reluctant to share individual teacher results and want the analysis to focus on the aggregate performance of the group. Some use the results to identify questions that caused students difficulty so they can eliminate the questions. Many teams are not yet using the analysis of results to inform or improve professional practice.	The school has created a specific process to bring teachers together multiple times throughout the year to analyze results from team-developed common assessments, district assessments, and state or provincial and national assessments. Teams use the results to identify areas of concern and to discuss strategies for improving the results.	Teachers are hungry for information on student learning. Throughout the year, each member of a collaborative team receives information that illustrates the success of his or her students in achieving an agreed-upon essential standard on team-developed common assessments he or she helped create, in comparison to all the students attempting to achieve that same standard. Teachers use the results to identify the strengths and weaknesses in their individual practice, to learn from one another, to identify areas of curriculum proving problematic for students, to improve their collective capacity to help all students learn, and to identify students in need of intervention or enrichment. They also analyze results from district, state or provincial, and national assessments and use them to validate their team assessments.

Where Do We Go From Here? Worksheet
Turning Data Into Information

Indicator of a PLC at Work	What steps or activities must you initiate to create this condition in your school?	Who will be responsible for initiating or sustaining these steps or activities?	What is a realistic timeline for each step or phase of the activity?	What will you use to assess the effectiveness of your initiative?
Collaborative teams of teachers regard ongoing analysis of evidence of student learning as a critical element in the teaching and learning process. Teachers receive frequent and timely information regarding student achievement. They use that information to: • Respond to students who are experiencing difficulty • Enrich and extend the learning of students who are proficient • Inform and improve the individual and collective practice of team members • Identify team professional development needs • Measure progress toward team goals				

Figure 6.1: Turning data into information continuum.

*Visit **go.SolutionTree.com/PLCbooks** for a free reproducible version of this figure.*

is an enormous difference between those for whom "assessment results are used primarily to report on student progress rather than to improve professional practice" (DuFour et al., 2016, p. 151) and those in which:

> Teachers use the results [of assessments] to identify the strengths and weaknesses in their individual practice, to learn from one another, to identify areas of curriculum proving problematic for students, to improve their collective capacity to help all students, and to identify students in need of intervention or enrichment. (DuFour et al., 2016, p. 151)

Let's return to the question skeptical teachers, administrators, and parents pose: "How do we know that this idea will work in our schools with our students?" Equipped with both student performance (effect) indicators and the degree of implementation of the proposed intervention (cause) indicators, the state provides not a hierarchical, authority-mandated response, but a learning response based on the reality of each school's choice from the state's level 2 menu. While states can and should serve as a filter for determining what goes on the menu—along with known school improvement best practices—state-level leaders should be the architects of a discernment process. Districts and schools must do more than merely adopt a program. They must be publicly accountable for how deeply they implement a process of continuous, collective adult learning.

The price of district discretion is transparency. For example, if a district wants to adopt innovative collaboration models by linking singleton teachers with colleagues outside the district to develop common assessments, interventions, and enrichment opportunities, they are free to do so. But discretion takes place within the boundary of transparent collaboration. If districts and schools want to experiment with different formative assessment methods, they are free to do so only as long as they transparently share the content and methodology of the assessments. Moreover, states can elevate focus over fragmentation by requiring schools and districts to choose only a few instructional initiatives and then monitor and report the details and degree of their implementation of each one.

The price of district discretion is transparency.

Level 2 accountability also allows the state to test its own hypotheses about the relationship between its school district requirements and the state's target outcomes. For example, many states have adopted extensive and burdensome teacher evaluation systems. The operating hypothesis appears to be that if teachers excel in each element of these evaluations, then student achievement will increase. That's a straightforward and testable hypothesis. A simple two-bar graph comparing the results of teachers with the highest ratings in each indicator to teachers with lower ratings should reveal the impact, if any, of each indicator on student achievement.

Similarly, state-mandated school-improvement plans represent a hypothesis that compliance with each plan element leads to improved student results. In an analysis of more than two thousand school plans, Douglas (Reeves, 2011) compares compliance with each element of the plan with student results. Over three years, some elements, such as using specific and measurable goals, are strongly related to student achievement. But other plan elements—to which administrators and teachers devote exceptional amounts of time—are unrelated or inversely related to student achievement (Reeves, 2011). The wise use of level 2 accountability indicators leads to a reduction, not an increase, of state mandates, so teachers and administrators should relentlessly focus on the professional practices that produce the greatest gains in student achievement.

Teachers and administrators should relentlessly focus on the professional practices that produce the greatest gains in student achievement.

Level 3: Putting It All Together

In order for accountability to positively contribute to a learning system, students, teachers, and administrators must be able to draw inferences about the relationship between the first two levels. In the past, the complexities of state testing and especially value-added accountability systems made deep analysis the exclusive province of research analysts far away from any classroom. But there is middle ground between the exceedingly complex variance-covariance matrices of some systems and facile assertions about education interventions (for example, "We tried that, and it didn't work").

Level 1 identifies the goal—improvements in student achievement. Level 2 describes the degree to which educators implement teaching and leadership practices that they hypothesize will lead to level 1 improvements. Level 3 sheds light on whether educators should continue, abandon, modify, or implement education practices to a greater degree.

It is possible that, if an intervention is sufficiently effective, then deeper implementation will be associated with better student results. Figure 6.2 shows a simple graph expressing this belief. Using the continuum language in figure 6.1 (pages 94–95), one might hypothesize that as teacher teams progress from *pre-initiating* to *initiating, implementing, developing,* and *sustaining,* each progression in professional practices brings improved student results.

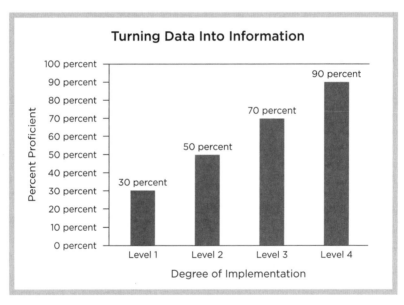

Figure 6.2: Turning data into information.

It is also possible that the intervention is completely ineffective, so gains from the intervention never materialize (see figure 6.3).

Most people recoil from such a finding, believing that whatever group of administrators and teachers who thought the XYZ Literary Program was a good idea is crazy, incompetent, or both. But wait a minute. No one intentionally chooses to harm students or waste the

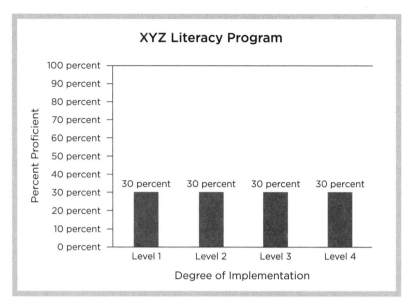

Figure 6.3: XYZ Literacy Program.

time of busy teachers. Most every initiative begins with good intentions. The reason school leaders succumb to the law of initiative fatigue (Reeves, 2006) is that they rarely engage in level 3 analysis, in which they systematically compare their hypotheses with the actual results. While corporate CEOs and education leaders are fond of talking about the value of failure, few people are actually rewarded for failure, even when—as is the case in this example—people and the organization they serve learn from that failure.

Most every initiative begins with good intentions.

There is a third possibility. In this example (see figure 6.4, page 100), a school implements the ABC Achievement Initiative and, ultimately, relates the initiative to improved student achievement results. But rather than the neat linear progression like in figure 6.2, the progression is nonlinear, with *gains in achievement occurring only at the deepest level of implementation.*

This phenomenon—in which educators associate only the deepest levels of implementation with significant gains in student performance— occurs with academic improvement initiatives as well as with

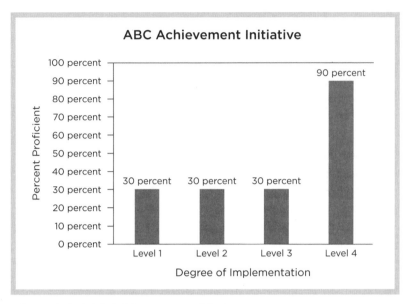

Figure 6.4: ABC Achievement Initiative.

Unless you are willing to implement an education initiative at the deepest level, then don't bother.

behavioral and engagement initiatives (Reeves, 2011). If that is what level 3 analysis suggests, then teachers and administrators learn a valuable lesson: unless you are willing to implement an education initiative at the deepest level, then don't bother.

State Accountability Policy as a Learning System

Imagine that schools and districts statewide collect information such as that in figures 6.2–6.4. During the first year of the new accountability system, one would expect wide variation among schools and districts as they employ different strategies to pursue the state's level 1 objectives. But with each passing year, schools should be able to ask, "What have the schools that face similar challenges to our school done? Which schools had the best performance? Which implementation strategies were most effective?"

Responding to ESSA with new accountability measures probably seems like a lot of work. After all, it's not that difficult to simply report annual test scores. The burdens of collaboration include listening, learning, and most problematic of all, changing and improving professional practices in order to meet the needs of students. We readily acknowledge that the PLC process is challenging for many schools in which collaboration has been an alien notion, and nearly every teacher and administrator has always received superior evaluations. Nevertheless, our experience is that the work of effective collaboration is far less burdensome, and far more meaningful and rewarding, than the work entailed in endless repetition of the cycle of annual test scores, disjointed initiatives, fragmentary implementation, and ultimate abandonment of those initiatives. Long-term success depends on a commitment to abiding professional practices of the sort that we have seen in the United States and around the world when schools make a commitment to the collaborative processes we outline in this book.

Experimentation and flexibility offer the potential for great innovation, but they may also present some risks and unintended consequences.

Risks and Rewards of State Innovation

After studying centuries of creativity and innovation, researchers believe the path to improvements in science, medicine, the arts, and yes—education—requires a high tolerance for error (Csikszentmihalyi, 1996; Grant, 2016). Visit any art museum from the Uffizi Gallery in Florence, Italy, to your local community museum and you won't see the canvases that Monet discarded or the sculptures that Michelangelo smashed. Listen to a great symphony and you might hear the majestic opening—think of the opening four notes of Beethoven's Symphony no. 5—but you will never hear the awful, awkward, meandering, and pedantic phrases from the preliminary drafts of a great work.

Similarly, in education, some observers envision great teaching and leadership as if they are great works of art—magically produced by innately gifted masters rather than professional labor developed over years of trial and error. Some education leaders talk of looking for talented teachers and leaders perhaps because they are unwilling to acknowledge that Geoff Colvin (2010) is right when he claims that talent is overrated. We've never seen an education conference promise,

"Dreadfully hard work, blood, sweat, tears, and lots of mistakes—a guaranteed good time!"

To the point of this chapter, state policymakers may ask, "When was the last time we awarded a contract to an organization that promised lots of trial and error and lots of errors before success?" If the answer is *never*, then you will not have risk-takers like Beethoven in education policy discussions.

What does this mean in the context of accountability policy? It means that it must be safe for teachers and administrators to report in their accountability documents, "We tried this idea, and it was not related to improved student achievement." Accountability policy will not be a learning system if the only evidence is happy talk and endless successes. It is vital for leaders and policymakers to learn what does *not* work. They can only reveal that information in an environment where they can discuss failure openly and without fear of retribution. We are not condoning reckless failure but rather those efforts made in good faith that, upon further reflection and consideration of the evidence, are not related to improved student results.

It is vital for leaders and policymakers to learn what does not work.

The easiest path for state policymakers in the wake of ESSA is to listen diligently to all stakeholders and then implement policies the legislature, governor, or state board of education wishes to implement. These accountability systems will show that education is a complete failure, a wonderful success, or somewhere in between. But what these traditional systems will *not* do is provide the engine of innovation—accompanied by hypothesis generation, testing, failure, and learning—essential for sustained education improvement. The greatest ESSA opportunity for state policymakers is a shift from *effect* data (typically, test scores) to *cause* data—measurable activities of teachers and administrators that lead to systematic improvements in student learning.

In the future, teachers, school and district leaders, and policymakers can, for example, compare the use of end-of-year, high-stakes tests with the impact of formative assessments. They can consider not merely data on school climate and student engagement but also data on the community, leadership, teaching, and student activities most and least associated with improved climate and engagement. But they will only be able to consider these alternative indicators if state policymakers are willing to take risks and endure the inevitable errors that risk requires.

Previous legislative attempts to improve teacher quality focused largely on the effects of what teachers did or failed to do in the classroom, as measured by their students' test scores. This flies in the face of thousands of studies (DuFour & Reeves, 2016; Hattie, 2009; Marzano, Pickering, & Pollock, 2001) that make it clear it is the quality of the classroom teacher, not his or her students' short-term test scores, that has the greatest influence on student achievement. However, *quality* will remain an elusive term unless and until state accountability policies define with precision not merely what processes, initiatives, and strategies to use, *but also articulate a continuum of implementation for each of them.*

> *It is the quality of the classroom teacher, not his or her students' short-term test scores, that has the greatest influence on student achievement.*

In sum, the risk of innovation in education accountability is that it is difficult and at times embarrassing. This carries political and personal risk. The rewards are what every education reform since the founding of the United States' first public school desires—real improvements in student learning.

Unintended Consequences of State Policies

Although the potential for improvement through experimentation and learning is enormous as a result of ESSA, there may also be unintended consequences such as the following that state policymakers would be wise to consider.

Additional Standards

It is counterintuitive that a law designed to relieve schools of many burdensome standards may actually lead to *additional* standards. Nevertheless, state policymakers should expect advocacy for subjects neglected by NCLB testing regimes, such as music, visual arts, drama, and athletics, as well as libraries, consumer finance, vocational education, technology, and many others. Lessons of the past teach that if it's not part of the testing and accountability machine, then it doesn't get noticed. As libraries are closed and arts programs decimated, state policymakers should expect a strong push at both the legislative and administrative levels to include new mandatory standards in these fields and others, as advocates seek to retake the ground lost during the years when all that mattered were test scores in mathematics and literacy.

Discontinuity Between Tests and Curriculum

Although it might be difficult to find many people to say a kind word about NCLB, one of the law's virtues was the stipulation that tests align with state standards. That is, students are tested for their understanding of the curriculum based on the standards of that state. ESSA, by contrast, allows states to adopt the commercially sponsored, norm-referenced tests that are, to put it charitably, unlikely to relate to the full range of school curricula.

It is worthwhile to recall the fundamental differences between *norm-referenced tests*, which report student performance in comparison to other students, and *standards-referenced tests*, which report student performance relative to a standard. For norm-referenced tests, 49 percent of students always score below average; but for standards-referenced tests, it is possible for 10 percent or 90 percent of students to be proficient. If teachers exhibit a genuine commitment to the achievement of standards measured against an objective scale of proficiency, then it's possible that a few, or many, students will be proficient. The Federal Aviation Administration, for example, administers a flight test to pilots, and the vast majority pass and an even higher proportion land the aircraft safely. The reason is that well before the flight test, the pilots have been prepared to succeed. The gap between rhetoric and reality is clearly apparent when policymakers exhort teachers and schools to meet high standards but then report test results that fail to reflect performance on those standards.

Uninformative Assessments

Although ESSA allows states to use a series of interim assessments, these new tests may be inappropriately labeled *formative* simply because they are not summative. That is, the assessment is a final test at the end of the year. However, the essence of a formative assessment is not the test itself, but how you use it. Formative assessments earn their name because they *inform* teaching and learning. Thus, an effective state accountability system would consider not merely the scores on interim assessments but the manner in which you use those results to identify students in need of immediate interventions or extensions, and to improve teaching and leadership decisions.

> *The essence of a formative assessment is not the test itself, but how you use it.*

Unexpected Pathways to Teacher and Leadership Certification

Although the commitment to placing highly qualified teachers in classrooms is hardly new, ESSA eliminates the requirement that teacher evaluation be tied to student growth. This may open the doors to some aspirants to the teaching profession. Others have seen education as an impossible game to win since 2001, with the vagaries of politicized and uninformed education policymaking.

An historic number of baby boomers retiring is compounding the shortage of teachers and administrators. Not only is there a teacher shortage in traditionally hard-to-fill fields, such as special education, English as a second language, and science, but also qualified and experienced administrators are increasingly hard to find (Maxwell, 2014). The increasing demand for teachers and administrators and the accompanying reluctance of teaching candidates to participate in a traditional career preparation model may lead to an avalanche of new paths to teacher certification and, in fact, may disrupt the entire notion of certification as a requirement of entry into the profession.

States should prepare for traditional teacher preparation institutions to strengthen their role as gatekeepers, potentially limiting innovation. They also should prepare for a wave of online programs that will change undergraduate teacher preparation in ways that mirror changes to many traditional masters and doctoral programs. That is, they produce credentials without meaningful field experience and effective preparation for the real world of teaching and education leadership.

In the next chapter, we turn our attention to what educators can expect on the path moving forward, illustrating how this new vision of education accountability can serve state policymakers as well as classroom teachers, building principals, and district leaders.

CHAPTER 7

The Path Ahead for ESSA

The road ahead for education accountability in the ESSA era offers three strikingly different paths. The first is a U-turn, taking us backward. The second is a series of switchbacks, taking schools and students in first one direction and then another. The third path, the one we hope states, districts, and schools will take, forges a new trail applying the best evidence of what we know can lead to excellence and equity for every student in every school.

The U-Turn

On the road ahead for education, some states will take a U-turn, and state education officials will continue with faulty assumptions and ineffective practices of the past. These policymakers cling to these practices which, using voluminous documentation and onerous requirements, attempt to intimidate teachers, administrators, and students into better performance. These policymakers persist in ranking teachers and schools based on a single annual assessment and measurements of Byzantine complexity. With each change of leadership or political affiliation, they move the goalposts so no one in the education system understands what being successful requires.

They also pursue every shiny new object in the education world and avoid tried-and-tested professional practices that seem too boring and insufficiently glitzy to gain attention. They prioritize political agendas, such as persistent attempts to prove the failure of public education by denying adequate funding, providing ambiguous leadership, and labeling schools and teachers as failures without establishing a constructive system for improvement.

The U-turn states regress to RTTT and NCLB failures, tolerating educational opportunities that are inherently unequal and bad practices, all in the name of local control. The standard of success in these states will not provide opportunities for *all* students to learn at high levels, but it will satisfy politically powerful constituents. The consequence may very well be cynical teachers and demotivated students.

Switchbacks

The roads up a mountain pass often use switchbacks—the back-and-forth paths that avoid the steep grade but add many more miles to the trip. Switchbacks in education policy are the result of changing tests, changing standards, and endlessly changing accountability measurements. The primary symptom of switchback states is the nearly universal expression from teachers that "this too shall pass." This kind of continual change stifles the intellectual and emotional investment required to make significant progress, because those who proceed in good faith with the changes of one leader quickly find themselves isolated and out of step with the next leader.

Switchbacks in education policy are the result of changing tests, changing standards, and endlessly changing accountability measurements.

Blogger Daarel Burnette II (2016) reports that in 2015, the chief state school officer changed in thirty-one states, plus there was a turnover of almost one-fifth of the country's state school board members. Only seven states saw no changes in education leadership. Leadership transiency is particularly acute among the most challenged schools and districts, with annual changes in leadership denying students and teachers the opportunity for the consistency and focus essential for sustained improvements in teaching and learning.

A New Path

Although ESSA offers the opportunity for a new path—one toward sustained educational excellence—policymakers may not choose it. This path requires the steadfast pursuit of improvement in every school, from those that struggle academically to those that enjoy high achievement according to traditional accountability measures. It requires leadership that elevates principles over politics and balances the need for clear policy priorities and local innovation. Specifically, states and school districts that pursue the new path will adhere to the following five principles.

> *It requires leadership that elevates principles over politics and balances the need for clear policy priorities and local innovation.*

1. **They will establish a moral imperative for change that transcends changes in leadership and political affiliation:** While politics and politicians change, moral imperatives endure. Fullan (2011b) contrasts moral imperatives with the *wrong drivers* of compliance and threats. The pursuit of a moral imperative demands deep commitment and intellectual consistency. It is inconsistent, for example, for state leaders to complain about unwarranted federal intrusions into education policy and then, given discretion to pursue a new path, freeze up until they have guidance from the federal government. Similarly, we call on district leaders to act *now* to establish effective accountability policies and not wait for their state departments to establish final regulations. The question is not "What does the higher authority want?" but rather "What is the right thing to do?"

2. **They will provide clear boundaries for professional practices:** In this book, we present compelling evidence that the PLC process provides the organizing framework for effective teaching, leadership, and learning. PLCs are not something that a school and district does for a year or two but rather represent the never-ending, continuous process of improvement through a collaborative focus on the four

critical questions of learning, assessment, intervention, and extension. We provide quantitative evidence and qualitative observations that establish PLCs as the best way to identify and replicate effective education practices. In the context of ESSA, states and districts can monitor the degree to which each school uses team-developed common formative assessments, data analysis, SMART goals, and explicit improvements in teaching practices.

3. **They will require transparency:** This is what Rick and Becky call *a transition from private practice to public practice.* The obligation of transparency requires, for example, that members of each collaborative team analyze frequent data on student achievement, and that they identify and observe specific teaching practices in order to reveal the most effective practices.

The least helpful statistics are district and school averages. We value and support teacher professionalism and academic freedom. Rick, after all, was a union president during his teaching career and argued passionately on behalf of respect for the professionalism of teachers. However, no profession is immune from observation and the expectation for improvement. Teachers, along with physicians, pilots, attorneys, engineers, and other professionals, pursue their craft in a public setting, sharing successes and failures so their experiences benefit every colleague and every student.

> *We value and support teacher professionalism and academic freedom.*

4. **They will require tolerance for risk and error, provided that the entire system has the opportunity to learn from errors:** Student engagement strategies that have been effective in the past may or may not work in the future. Research continues to reveal best practices in assessment and data analysis. The very nature of improvement requires that educators acknowledge there is room to improve and

that the best practices today yield to even better practices tomorrow. Teachers and administrators are on the right path when they can say, "We tried this strategy, but the results from our students suggest that there is a better way to reach them." They know that a zero-risk environment is a zero-learning environment and, therefore, routinely taking the risks and making the mistakes are inherent parts of innovation.

> *Routinely taking the risks and making the mistakes are inherent parts of innovation.*

5. **They will acknowledge that accountability is no longer a means to label and intimidate teachers, students, schools, and districts:** Rather, accountability is an essential element of a learning system, moving from individual anecdotes of practice to systemic change. The role of state and district leaders is no longer to report the data but to draw inferences from it, replicating the most effective practices and repealing demands for practices unrelated to student achievement.

A learning system should be distinguished not only by what it requires but also by what it does *not* require. Therefore, while effective learning systems require collaboration and transparency, they also withdraw requirements for burdensome documentation in school-improvement plans, teacher-evaluation systems, and other regulations that compete with effective practices for the time, attention, and energy of teachers and school administrators.

> *A learning system should be distinguished not only by what it requires but also by what it does not require.*

The new path is possible and many schools are already pursuing it, but not because it's required. They are doing so because *it is the right thing to do*. These schools are examples of continuous professional learning that every state, every district, and every school should pursue—if only they have the courage to do so.

What to Do Now

W e have had the pleasure of visiting literally thousands of amazingly effective classrooms. We've noticed that, when students enter these classrooms, they do not see a notice on the board that contains the words, "Suggested next steps" or "If you get around to it, and you are completely comfortable, and you don't have anything else occupying your attention, then you might consider the following . . ." No, the great teachers in these classrooms write two simple words on the board to gain the attention of their students: *Do Now*. It is in the spirit of these amazing teachers that we offer our Do Now list.

- **Learn what your school, district, and state is doing to respond to ESSA:** If the response is a tepid recycling of failed accountability policies—test scores, obscure ratings, and no consideration of the underlying causes of student success or failure—then challenge it. There are two underlying causes of student success and failure. The most commonly considered causes are demographic factors, such as family socioeconomic status and the long-term results of poverty and discrimination. It is also essential, however, to consider causes that are within the control of school leaders. These include curriculum, assessment, teaching practices, and leadership policies.

No matter your political perspective or that of your colleagues, community, and school board, remember that ESSA was bipartisan legislation in which both major political parties agreed to reject the micromanagement of the past in favor of the innovation of the future. Even if your state has already submitted a plan for ESSA implementation, the law explicitly requires input from every stakeholder, including every reader of this book. It's not too late to provide your input to your local and state officials right now.

- **Request that your school and district become a "model innovation system" for your state:** Even if state officials have already submitted their ESSA compliance plan, there remains room for schools and districts to become the engines of innovation. The perspective of these proposed innovations is not to escape accountability, but to make accountability more meaningful and effective. This approach says to state and federal policymakers, "We do not fear accountability, but we insist that accountability can be a learning system. Let us show you how it can be done."

- **Start now if your school system is not yet engaged in professional learning communities as the fundamental organizing structure and culture for your faculty and leadership:** If your school system already is engaged in the PLC process, then resolve to systematically observe and hold yourselves accountable for the effective implementation of the PLC at Work framework.

In the end, our claim is not that if you follow a set formula, you will find easy success. To paraphrase President John F. Kennedy's challenge when he encouraged the nation to literally shoot for the moon, our challenge is not to engage in this process because it easy, but because it is hard (National Aeronautics and Space Administration, Software Robotics and Simulation Division, n.d.). The challenges of effective professional collaboration and redefining education accountability are immense, but the rewards are even greater. If the Every Student Succeeds Act were repealed tomorrow, we would nevertheless still advocate the ideas in this book. So please choose the practices that are proven to work and do them. Do them now.

Sample School-Level Accountability Indicators

E SSA provides great opportunities for innovative school and district accountability indicators. In this appendix, you will find samples of school-level indicators. The purpose of these indicators is to allow teachers, leaders, and community members to better understand the relationship between the actions of teachers and leaders and student achievement.

The key to effectively using this appendix is the phrase *menus, not mandates*. Schools should have no more than six or seven school-based indicators, and they should select indicators based on the needs of the students in each school. Thus, it is unlikely that every school in a district will have the same school-level indicators. However, every school has the same overall goals with regard to academic achievement, equity, safety, and other key system-level objectives.

Classroom teachers and administrators suggest each of these indicators. There is a mix of academic indicators as well as student and parent indicators. This appendix is divided into the following areas.

- Reading
- Writing

- Language

- Speaking

- Mathematics

- Science

- Arts

- Study skills

- Technology

- School and community service

- Parent involvement

- Safety and climate

- School completion

Despite the promise of ESSA to encourage innovation, you should expect some resistance to new accountability indicators. Consider, for example, the following scenario.

The board president was shocked and upset to learn that the Accountability Task Force had recommended that the local school committees would be choosing the school-based indicators in the new accountability system. "They'll just give themselves softballs!" the president lamented.

While this concern is understandable, our experience suggests that trusting local educators and leaders to select school-based accountability indicators is a wise policy. Rather than easy-to-accomplish "softball" goals, school-based indicators tend to be creative, relevant, and challenging. Moreover, the architecture of a comprehensive accountability system offers an automatic check to discourage easy goals and encourage challenging indicators at the school level.

If the published accountability report shows that on systemwide indicators a substantial number of students are not meeting state and district standards, but the school-based indicators suggest that everything is rosy because superficial and easy goals have been attained, then the school leadership clearly lacks credibility. If, on the other hand, the school goals are aggressive, challenging, and substantive, then it will be clear to stakeholders and policymakers reading the accountability report that the school leadership is aggressively pursuing improved student achievement (Reeves, 2004).

Following are some sample school-level accountability indicators.

Reading

A version of this text was originally published in Accountability in Action: A Blueprint for Learning Organizations *(2nd ed.) (Reeves, 2004). Used with permission.*

Increase the percentage of students (specify a particular group) who score at or above the state standard on the grade 3 (or other grade level) reading comprehension test.

Increase the percentage of students (specify a particular group) who meet or exceed the district goal for reading scores.

Increase the percentage of students who are at or above grade level, as measured by informal or formal criterion-referenced reading assessments.

Increase the percentage of students who are reading at or above grade level, as measured by the district reading test.

Increase the percentage of students (specify a particular group) performing at or above expected grade or age level in reading on a district-approved reading test.

Increase the percentage of students performing at or above expected grade or age level on a teacher-made language arts assessment.

Increase the percentage of students who are able to read and pronounce basic vocabulary words for reading, as reported by teacher observation.

Increase the percentage of students who are able to use letter or sound relationships to phonetically decode words while reading.

Increase the percentage of students who are able to use context clues to decode unfamiliar words.

Increase the percentage of students who are at or above grade level, as measured by reading readiness scores.

Decrease the number of students whose primary language is other than English who are reading one year or more below grade level.

Increase the number of students who read (specify number) of books and share something they learned orally, artistically, musically, or by doing a multimedia presentation.

Increase the amount of material available for student reading in classrooms or the school library or media center.

Increase the number of students involved in project-based reading assignments.

Writing

Increase the percentage of students (specify a particular group) who meet or exceed the district goal on a district writing performance assessment.

Increase the percentage of students who publish their own books and achieve a score of proficient or better on a related performance assessment.

Increase the percentage of students performing at or above expected grade or age level in writing, as demonstrated through student portfolios.

Increase the percentage of students who use word processing to satisfactorily complete writing assignments.

Increase the percentage of students involved in writing portfolio conferences, based on portfolio guidelines.

Increase the number of students involved in project-based writing assignments.

Increase the percentage of classes that use writing performance assessment portfolios.

Increase the number of writing samples scored by someone other than the student's classroom teacher.

Language

Increase the percentage of students (specify a particular group) performing at or above expected grade or age level in oral language, as reported by their teacher.

Increase the percentage of students (specify a particular group) performing at or above expected grade or age level in language using performance assessments.

Increase the percentage of students who speak a language other than English as their primary language who score at the proficient or higher level on an English proficiency test.

Increase the number of students involved in project-based language assignments.

Speaking

Increase the percentage of students who achieve a score of proficient or higher on an oral communication performance assessment.

Increase the number of students involved in project-based public speaking assignments.

Increase the percentage of students who achieve a score of proficient or higher on a public speaking performance assessment.

Increase the percentage of students who achieve a score of proficient or higher on a teacher-made public speaking assessment.

Mathematics

Increase the percentage of students (specify a particular group) who score at or above the proficient level on a grade 4 (or other grade level) mathematics assessment.

Increase the percentage of students who achieve a score of proficient or higher on a mathematics performance assessment.

Increase the percentage of students who achieve a score of proficient or higher on a teacher-made computation test.

Increase the percentage of students who achieve a score of proficient or higher on a mathematical problem-solving test.

Increase the percentage of students who achieve a proficient or higher score on a calculator proficiency performance assessment.

Increase the percentage of students who achieve a score of proficient or higher on a performance assessment that evaluates their ability to use computer-generated charts and graphs to solve real-world mathematics problems.

Increase the percentage of students who correctly use manipulatives in mathematics, as observed by the teacher.

Increase the percentage of students who achieve a score of proficient or higher on a problem-solving performance assessment.

Increase the percentage of students involved in projects using mathematical principles in collaboration with community or business partners, and who achieve a score of proficient or higher on a school-based performance assessment.

Increase the percentage of students who meet or exceed the district goal on an external test of mathematics achievement.

Increase the percentage of students who are at or above grade level, as measured by a mathematics readiness test.

Increase the percentage of students (specify a particular group) performing at or above expected grade level or age in mathematics, as demonstrated through student portfolios.

Increase the percentage of students (specify a particular group) performing at or above grade level in mathematics.

Increase the percentage of classes that use mathematics performance assessment portfolios.

Science

Increase the percentage of students who participate in a science fair that requires a hypothesis, experiment, and conclusions.

Increase the percentage of students (specify a particular group) who receive a proficient or higher score on a district science performance assessment.

Increase the percentage of students who achieve a score of proficient or higher on a district science performance assessment.

Increase the percentage of students who achieve a score of proficient or higher on a scientific problem-solving performance assessment.

Increase the number of hours of science instruction facilitated in science laboratories or classrooms.

Increase the percentage of students who use manipulatives in science, as observed by the teacher.

Increase the percentage of students who achieve a score of proficient or higher on a teacher-constructed test of scientific knowledge and skills.

Increase the number of science activities that involve community or business partnerships.

Increase the number of hours of science instruction provided by certified science teachers.

Increase the amount of laboratory and other equipment available for science experiments.

Increase the number of outdoor field experiments or visits to science museums and scientific points of interest.

Increase participation in collaborative university- or college-sponsored science programs and projects.

Increase the percentage of students who score proficient or higher on writing-to-learn science performance assessments.

Increase the percentage of students (specify a particular group) who can use the scientific method to solve real-world science problems or issues.

Increase the percentage of students involved in community or school-based projects that involve environmental hypotheses, data collection, and conclusions.

Increase the percentage of students who use computers to access and use information from science-related websites.

Arts

Increase the percentage of students who participate in art classes or art instruction.

Increase the percentage of students who participate in music programs and music performances

Increase the percentage of students who participate in dance programs and dance performances.

Increase the percentage of students who complete art projects for public display or presentation.

Increase the number of art-related activities that involve community or business partners.

Increase the percentage of students who achieve a score of proficient or higher on an art portfolio, musical performance, dramatic presentation, dance, or other artistic expression.

Study Skills

Increase the percentage of students who achieve a score of proficient or higher on a time management performance assessment.

Increase the percentage of students who prepare and regularly use a study schedule, as reported by the teacher.

Increase the percentage of students who demonstrate their ability to use effective reading habits.

Increase the percentage of students who take notes while they read to improve their overall comprehension.

Increase the percentage of students who demonstrate their ability to take effective classroom notes from lectures or whole-group activities.

Increase the percentage of students who demonstrate effective test-taking strategies.

Increase the percentage of students who demonstrate their ability to use SQ3R (Survey, Question, Read, Recite, Review) or other before-during-after strategies to read textbooks effectively, as measured by reading performance assessments.

Increase the percentage of students who achieve a score of proficient or higher on a teacher-made study skills performance assessment.

Technology

Increase the percentage of computer-proficient students who demonstrate all the skills listed on a schoolwide computer assessment checklist.

Increase the total percentage of assessments administered using computers.

Increase the percentage of students who successfully complete a keyboarding performance assessment.

Increase the number of students who increase their keyboarding speed from _____ words per minute to _____ words per minute.

Increase the percentage of students who score proficient or higher on a computer usage performance assessment.

Increase the percentage of students who demonstrate their ability to log on to, access, and download information from websites.

Increase the percentage of students using the Internet, electronic data searches, and so on, for research.

Increase the percentage of students who complete a technology portfolio with a score of proficient or higher.

Increase the number of multimedia projects that students complete using technology.

Increase the number of word-processed products included in writing portfolios.

School and Community Service

Increase the number of hours that students volunteer in the community.

Increase the number of business or community partnership activities that link classroom learning with real-world issues and problems.

Increase the number of community service or career awareness projects undertaken by the school.

Increase the percentage of students who participate in student government, advisory councils, or other similar activities.

Increase the number of students who achieve a score of proficient or higher on a social studies or global awareness assessment.

Increase the number of adult mentor and tutor contacts with students.

Increase the percentage of students (specify a particular group or age/grade level) who participate in school-to-work activities.

Increase the percentage of students who use academics to operate student-run school businesses.

Parent Involvement

Increase the percentage of parents who participate in the parent-teacher conferences.

Increase the number of parent volunteer hours.

Increase the number of parent activities offered at the school.

Increase the number of parents who log on to the school website to access information about their children's performance.

Increase the number of parents who utilize the school's parent resource room.

Increase the number of parents who attend school- or district-sponsored workshops.

Increase the number of parents who attend back-to-school nights.

Increase the number of parents who pick up their children's report cards at the school.

Safety and Climate

Increase the percentage of students who ride the school bus without bus complaints.

Increase the percentage of students who receive "good bus rider" incentive awards.

Increase the percentage of students who do not receive lunchroom complaints.

Increase the percentage of students who receive "good lunchroom behavior" incentive awards.

Increase the percentage of students who receive positive school recognition for following school rules.

Increase the percentage of students who achieve a score of proficient or higher on a peer mediation performance assessment.

Increase the number of students who participate in school-sponsored conflict resolution or reduction workshops.

School Completion

Increase the percentage of students (specify a particular group) who remain enrolled from grade to grade, controlled for student mobility.

Increase the percentage of students who demonstrate their mastery of requisite standards by being promoted to the next grade.

APPENDIX B

Sample System-Level Accountability Indicators

System-level accountability indicators reflect the goals of the entire system. While school-based indicators reflect the individual needs of each school, system-level indicators reflect the shared values of the entire community and, therefore, apply to every school. District-level administrators suggest these sample system-level accountability indicators.

The indicators include the following areas of performance.

- Academic performance
- Attendance
- Teacher effectiveness
- Equity
- Stakeholder satisfaction
- Safety

Academic Performance

A version of this text was originally published in Accountability in Action: A Blueprint for Learning Organizations *(2nd ed.) (Reeves, 2004). Used with permission.*

Percentage of _____-grade students who have been enrolled since (specify time period) who score at or above the proficient level on the district _____-grade reading (or other subject area) test

Percentage of _____-grade students who score at or above the proficient level on the (specify test), as compared with the same students' scores from the previous year

Percentage of regular education students who have been in school since (specify time period) who score at or above the proficient level on the reading (or other subject area) subtest of the (specify test)

Percentage of regular education students who have been in school since (specify time period) who score at or above the proficient level on the reading (or other subject area) subtest of the (specify test), as compared with the same students' scores from the previous year

Percentage of students performing at or above the state standard in (specify subject area) on the (specify test)

Percentage of students performing at or above the proficient level on the district criterion-referenced reading (or other subject area) test

Percentage of students who read at or above grade or age level by the end of grade 3 before being promoted to grade 4, as measured by the (specify test)

Percentage of special education students who participate in state and district assessments with no accommodations, with appropriate accommodations, or with an alternative assessment consistent with the individualized education plan (IEP)

Percentage of special education students who participate in state and district testing, as compared with the percentage of students who participated the previous school year

Percentage of students who meet or exceed grade-level standards in reading, writing, mathematics, and science by _____ (specify time frame)

Percentage of students who have been in school since (specify time period) whose two ratings totaled 6 or more on the district 4-point rubric for writing assessment

Percentage of students who score at or above the proficient level on four out of five school-based writing assessments, as compared with the same students' scores from the previous year

Percentage of _____-grade students who have been in school since (specify time period) who receive a score of proficient or higher on the district science performance assessment

Percentage of _____-grade students with attendance rates of 90 percent or more and who have been in school since (specify time period) who score at or above the proficient level on the district performance assessment in (specify subject area)

Percentage of students who achieve a passing score on the eighth-grade proficiency examination required for continuation to high school

Percentage of students who achieve a passing score on the eighth-grade proficiency examination required for continuation to high school on the first trial

Percentage of students who achieve a passing score on the eighth-grade proficiency examination required for continuation to high school, as compared with the percentage of eighth graders who passed the examination the previous year

Percentage of high school seniors who demonstrate proficiency based on the district's writing assessments required for graduation; the district goal is _____ percent

Percentage of high school seniors who score at or above the proficient level on the district (specify subject area) assessment, as compared with scores of seniors from the previous year; the district goal is _____ percent

Percentage of students who demonstrate mastery of written and spoken expression by writing, presenting, and defending a clearly reasoned, persuasively argued research paper

Through participation in a group project that benefits the community, percentage of students who demonstrate the capacity to analyze a social issue from multiple points of view and to interact as a constructive member of a team

Percentage of students who demonstrate mastery of mathematical proficiency equivalent to three years of study beyond algebra 1

Percentage of students who demonstrate a high level of proficiency in science, equivalent to three years of high school study to include the physical, biological, and chemical sciences

Percentage of students who meet or exceed standards in core subject areas: English, mathematics, science, and social studies

Attendance

Percentage of students with attendance rates of _____ percent or higher

Percentage of students whose attendance rates meet or exceed district or school goals, as compared with the attendance rate from the previous year

Percentage of students with attendance rates of _____ percent or higher who attain a grade point average of at least _____

Increase in the school's overall grade point average, as compared with the grade point average from the previous year

Teacher Effectiveness

Percentage of students who participate in _____ hours of (specify subject area) instruction per week

Percentage of school's students taught by a teacher licensed in the appropriate grade level or subject area

Percentage of teachers who receive a score of proficient or higher on four out of five observations during the school year

Equity

Percentage of (specify target group) students who meet or exceed district standards in (specify subject area), as measured by the (specify test)

Percentage of (specify target group) students who earn at least _____ hours of credit in mathematics and science (or other subject area)

Percentage of (specify target group) students who achieve high school graduation rates at or above (specify percentage)

Percentage of (specify target group) students who enroll in advanced placement (AP) courses

Decrease in percentage of (specify target group) students who are suspended or expelled from school

Decrease in percentage of (specify target group) students who receive disciplinary referrals

Stakeholder Satisfaction

Percentage of parents who report that they are satisfied or very satisfied with their children's schools on a parent-satisfaction survey

Percentage of teachers who report that they are satisfied or very satisfied with their ability to help all students succeed at high levels on a teacher-satisfaction survey

Percentage of students who report that they are satisfied or very satisfied with the quality of the learning at their schools on a student-satisfaction survey

Safety

Number of violent acts committed against students by (target date)

Number of violent acts committed against teachers and staff by (target date)

Number of incidents involving violence, weapons, drugs, or alcohol

REFERENCES AND RESOURCES

Aldeman, C. (2015). School accountability before, during, and after NCLB. *Education Next.* Accessed at http://educationnext.org/school -accountability-before-during-and-after-nclb on March 3, 2016.

Álvarez, B. (2016, April 14). States "setting the table" for ESSA implementation. *NEA Today.* Accessed at http://neatoday.org/2016 /04/14/states-setting-table-for-essa-implementation on May 2, 2016.

American Academy of Pediatrics. (2014). *Let them sleep: AAP recommends delaying start times of middle and high schools to combat teen sleep deprivation.* Accessed at www.aap.org/en-us/about-the -aap/aap-press-room/Pages/Let-Them-Sleep-AAP-Recommends -Delaying-Start-Times-of-Middle-and-High-Schools-to-Combat -Teen-Sleep-Deprivation.aspx on May 29, 2017.

American Statistical Association. (2014). *ASA statement on using value-added models for educational assessment.* Accessed at www.scribd .com/doc/217916454/ASA-VAM-Statement-1 on January 30, 2015.

Amos, J. (2016). The graduation effect: Increasing national high school graduation rate key to job creation and economic growth, new Alliance analysis finds. *Straight A's: Public Education Policy and Progress, 16*(1). Accessed at http://all4ed.org/articles/the-graduation -effect-increasing-national-high-school-graduation-rate-key-to-job -creation-and-economic-growth-new-alliance-analysis-finds/ on June 4, 2017.

Association for Supervision and Curriculum Development. (2015). *Elementary and Secondary Education Act: Comparison of the No Child Left Behind Act to the Every Student Succeeds Act.* Accessed at www.ascd.org/ASCD/pdf/siteASCD/policy/ESEA_NCLB _ComparisonChart_2015.pdf on June 4, 2017.

Barber, M., & Mourshed, M. (2007). *How the world's best-performing school systems come out on top.* New York: McKinsey. Accessed at http://mckinseyonsociety.com/downloads/reports/Education /Worlds_School_Systems_Final.pdf on January 30, 2017.

Barber, M., & Mourshed, M. (2009). *Shaping the future: How good education systems can become great in the decade ahead—Report on the International Education Roundtable.* New York: McKinsey. Accessed at www.eurekanet.ru/res_ru/0_hfile_1906_1.pdf on January 30, 2017.

Blaustein, A. P., & Zangrando, R. L. (Eds.). (1991). *Civil rights and African Americans: A documentary history.* Evanston, IL: Northwestern University Press. (Original work published 1968)

Braun, H. I. (2005). *Using student progress to evaluate teachers: A primer on value-added models.* Princeton, NJ: Educational Testing Service. Accessed at www.ets.org/Media/Research/pdf/PICVAM.pdf on January 30, 2017.

Brown v. Board of Education, 347 U.S. 483 (1954).

Burnette II, D. (2016, February 16). *2015 saw historic shift in state education leadership, new report says* [Blog post]. Accessed at http:// blogs.edweek.org/edweek/state_edwatch/2016/02/across_the _nation_there_was.html on October 16, 2016.

Carey, K. (2015, January 24). A quiet revolution in helping lift the burden of student debt. *The New York Times.* Accessed at www .nytimes.com/2015/01/25/upshot/a-quiet-revolution-in-helping-lift -the-burden-of-student-debt.html?nlid=65639414&src=recpb&abt =0002&abg=1 on January 30, 2017.

Civic Impulse. (n.d.a). *H.R. 1 (107th): No Child Left Behind Act of 2001.* Accessed at www.govtrack.us/congress/bills/107/hr1 on June 8, 2017.

Civic Impulse. (n.d.b). *H.R. 1804 (103rd): Goals 2000: Educate America Act.* Accessed at www.govtrack.us/congress/bills/103 /hr1804 on June 7, 2017.

Colvin, G. (2010). *Talent is overrated: What really separates world-class performers from everybody else.* New York: Portfolio.

Commission on No Child Left Behind. (2007). *Beyond NCLB: Fulfilling the promise to our nation's children.* Washington, DC: Aspen Institute. Accessed at http://phetoolkit.net/docs/Aspen%20Commission%20on%20NCLB.pdf on May 27, 2017.

Conzemius, A., & O'Neill, J. (2014). *The Handbook for SMART school teams: Revitalizing best practices for collaboration* (2nd ed.). Bloomington, IN: Solution Tree Press.

Cook, G. (2016). Regulating the Every Student Succeeds Act. *Policy Priorities, 22*(2), 1–7.

Csikszentmihalyi, M. (1996). *Creativity: Flow and the psychology of discovery and invention.* New York: HarperCollins.

Dean, C. B., Hubbell, E. R., Pitler, H., & Stone, B. J. (2012). *Classroom instruction that works: Research-based strategies for increasing student achievement* (2nd ed.). Alexandria, VA: Association for Supervision and Curriculum Development.

DuFour, R. (2015). *In praise of American educators: And how they can become even better.* Bloomington, IN: Solution Tree Press.

DuFour, R., DuFour, R., & Eaker, R. (2008). *Revisiting Professional Learning Communities at Work: New insights for improving schools.* Bloomington, IN: Solution Tree Press.

DuFour, R., DuFour, R., Eaker, R., Many, T. W., & Mattos, M. (2016). *Learning by doing: A handbook for Professional Learning Communities at Work* (3rd ed.). Bloomington, IN: Solution Tree Press.

DuFour, R., & Fullan, M. (2013). *Cultures built to last: Systemic PLCs at Work.* Bloomington, IN: Solution Tree Press.

DuFour, R., & Reeves, D. B. (2016). The futility of PLC lite. *Phi Delta Kappan, 97*(6), 69–71.

Education Week. (2016). *Inside ESSA: The new federal K–12 law.* Bethesda, MD: Author.

Elementary and Secondary Education Act of 1965, Pub. L. No. 89–10, 20 U.S.C. § 6301 (1965).

Every Student Succeeds Act of 2015, Pub. L. No. 114–95, 20 U.S.C. § 1177 (2015).

FairTest. (2015). *Independent test results show NCLB fails.* Accessed at www.fairtest.org/independent-test-results-show-nclb-fails on March 21, 2015.

Franklin, C., Harris, M. B., & Allen-Meares, P. (Eds.). (2006). *The school services sourcebook: A guide for school-based professionals.* New York: Oxford University Press.

Friedman, L. (2003). *Brown v. Board of Education.* Accessed at http://americanradioworks.publicradio.org/features/marshall/friedman.html on April 24, 2016.

Fullan, M. (2010). *All systems go: The change imperative for whole system reform.* Thousand Oaks, CA: Corwin Press.

Fullan, M. (2011a). *Change leader: Learning to do what matters most.* San Francisco: Jossey-Bass.

Fullan, M. (2011b). *Choosing the wrong drivers for whole system reform.* East Melbourne, Australia: Center for Strategic Education. Accessed at http://michaelfullan.ca/wp-content/uploads/2016/06/13396088160.pdf on May 31, 2017.

Fullan, M. (2014). *Leadership: Maximizing impact.* Accessed at http://michaelfullan.ca/wp-content/uploads/2016/06/14_Spring_Maximizing-Impact-Handout.compressed.pdf on May 31, 2017.

Fullan, M., & Quinn, J. (2016). *Coherence: The right drivers in action for schools, districts, and systems.* Thousand Oaks, CA: Corwin Press.

Gardner, H. (2000). *The disciplined mind: Beyond facts and standardized tests, the K–12 education that every child deserves.* New York: Penguin.

Gardner, H. (2007). *Five minds for the future.* Boston: Harvard Business School Press.

Gewertz, C. (2016, March 22). State solidarity erodes on Common-Core tests. *Education Week.* Accessed at www.edweek.org/ew/articles/2016/03/23/state-solidarity-erodes-on-common-core-tests.html?qs=Common+Core+Assessments on July 10, 2016.

Goldstein, D. (2014). *The teacher wars: A history of America's most embattled profession.* New York: Doubleday.

Grant, A. M. (2016). *Originals: How non-conformists move the world.* New York: Viking.

Greenberg, J., McKee, A., & Walsh, K. (2013). *Teacher prep review: A review of the nation's teacher preparation programs—Executive summary.* Accessed at www.nctq.org/dmsView/Teacher_Prep _Review_executive_summary on January 22, 2015.

Gutowski, C., & Rado, D. (2014, August 6). Study shows many teachers not credentialed in their subjects. *Chicago Tribune.* Accessed at www.chicagotribune.com/news/ct-met-out-of-field-teachers -20140806-story.html on May 31, 2017.

Hargreaves, A., Boyle, A., & Harris, A. (2014). *Uplifting leadership: How organizations, teams, and communities raise performance.* San Francisco: Jossey-Bass.

Hargreaves, A., & Fullan, M. (2012). *Professional capital: Transforming teaching in every school.* New York: Teachers College Press.

Hattie, J. (2009). *Visible learning: A synthesis of over 800 meta-analyses relating to achievement.* London: Routledge.

Holmes Group. (1995). *Tomorrow's schools of education.* East Lansing, MI: Author. Accessed at http://files.eric.ed.gov/fulltext/ED399220 .pdf on January 30, 2017.

Howard, J. (1995). You can't get there from here: The need for a new logic in education reform. *Daedelus, 124*(4), 85–92.

Huetteman, E., & Rich, M. (2015, December 2). House restores local education control in revising No Child Left Behind. *The New York Times.* Accessed at www.nytimes.com/2015/12/03/us/house -restores-local-education-control-in-revising-no-child-left-behind .html?hp&action=click&pgtype=Homepage&clickSource=story -heading&module=second-column-region&region=top-news&WT .nav=top-news&_r=4 on May 2, 2016.

Ingersoll, R. M. (2007). A comparative study of teacher preparation and qualifications in six nations (Policy Brief No. RB-47). Accessed at www.cpre.org/sites/default/files/policybrief/887_rb47.pdf on March 21, 2015.

"A Jeffersonian compact": The statement by the president and governors. (1989, October 1). *The New York Times.* Accessed at http://query .nytimes.com/gst/fullpage.html?res=950DE7DB1330F932A35753 C1A96F948260&sec=&spon=&pagewanted=2 on January 30, 2017.

Jochim, A., & McGuinn, P. (2016). The politics of the Common Core assessments: Why states are quitting the PARCC and Smarter Balanced testing consortia. *EducationNext, 16*(4). Accessed at http:// educationnext.org/the-politics-of-common-core-assessments-parcc -smarter-balanced on May 31, 2017.

Klein, A. (2015a, December 2). *ESEA reauthorization coasts through House; next stop: U.S. Senate* [Blog post]. Accessed at http://blogs .edweek.org/edweek/campaign-k-12/2015/12/esea_reauthorization _coasts_th.html on May 2, 2016.

Klein, A. (2015b, April 10). No Child Left Behind: An overview. *Education Week.* Accessed at www.edweek.org/ew/section /multimedia/no-child-left-behind-overview-definition-summary .html on May 6, 2016.

Klein, A. (2016a, March 31). The Every Student Succeeds Act: An ESSA overview. *Education Week.* Accessed at www.edweek.org/ew/issues /every-student-succeeds-act/?cmp=eml-eb-popweek+04082016 on January 30, 2017.

Klein, A. (2016b, January 5). Under ESSA, states, districts to share more power. *Education Week.* Accessed at www.edweek.org/ew/articles /2016/01/06/under-essa-states-districts-to-share-more.html?cmp =eml-eb-sr-essa+011516 on May 31, 2017.

Layton, L. (2015, December 9). Senate overwhelmingly passes new education legislation. *The Washington Post.* Accessed at https:// washingtonpost.com/local/education/senate-overwhelmingly-passes -new-national-education-legislation/2015/12/09/be1b1f94-9d2a -11e5-a3c5-c77f2cc5a43c_story.html?utm_term=.7f5fbe7cd73b on March 22, 2017.

LBJ Presidential Library. (n.d.). *Johnson's remarks on signing the Elementary and Secondary Education Act.* Accessed at www .lbjlibrary.org/lyndon-baines-johnson/timeline/johnsons-remarks -on-signing-the-elementary-and-secondary-education-act on April 20, 2016.

Levine, A. (2006). *Educating school teachers.* Washington, DC: Education Schools Project.

Levine, A. (2013, June 21). Fixing how we train U.S. teachers. *The Hechinger Report.* Accessed at http://hechingerreport.org/fixing -how-we-train-u-s-teachers on January 31, 2015.

Marzano, R. J., Pickering, D. J., & Pollock, J. E. (2001). *Classroom instruction that works: Research-based strategies for increasing student achievement*. Alexandria, VA: Association for Supervision and Curriculum Development.

Maxwell, L. A. (2014, March 24). *Shortage of principals for school turnarounds, urban K–12 leaders say* [Blog post]. Accessed at http:// blogs.edweek.org/edweek/District_Dossier/2014/03/city_school _leaders_get.html on October 16, 2016.

McCaffrey, D. F., Lockwood, J. R., Koretz, D. M., & Hamilton, L. S. (2003). *Evaluating value-added models for teacher accountability*. Santa Monica, CA: RAND. Accessed at www.rand.org/pubs /monographs/2004/RAND_MG158.pdf on January 30, 2017.

Mehta, J. (2013, May/June). Why American education fails: And how lessons from abroad could improve it. *Foreign Affairs*. Accessed at www.foreignaffairs.com/articles/139113/jal-mehta/why-american -education-fails on January 30, 2017.

Murphy, J., Hallinger, P., & Heck, R. H. (2013). Leading via teacher evaluation: The case of the missing clothes? *Educational Researcher*, *42*(6), 349–354.

National Aeronautics and Space Administration, Software Robotics and Simulation Division. (n.d.). *John F. Kennedy moon speech: Rice Stadium*. Accessed at https://er.jsc.nasa.gov/seh/ricetalk.htm on June 17, 2017.

National Commission on Excellence in Education. (n.d.). *A nation at risk*. Accessed at www.ed.gov/pubs/NatAtRisk/risk.html on June 6, 2016.

National Governors Association Center for Best Practices & Council of Chief State School Officers. (2010a). *Common Core State Standards for mathematics*. Washington, DC: Authors. Accessed at www .corestandards.org/assets/CCSSI_Math%20Standards.pdf on March 23, 2017.

National Governors Association Center for Best Practices & Council of Chief State School Officers. (2010b). *Common Core State Standards initiative*. Accessed at www.corestandards.org/about-the-standards on March 23, 2017.

National Writing Project. (2010, April 14). *New report finds that writing can be powerful driver for improving reading skills*. Accessed at www .nwp.org/cs/public/print/resource/3126 on July 10, 2016.

No Child Left Behind Act of 2001, Pub. L. No. 107–110, 20 U.S.C. § 6319 (2002).

North Central Regional Educational Laboratory. (1994). *Summary of Goals 2000: Educate America Act.* Accessed at www.ncrel.org/sdrs /areas/issues/envrnmnt/stw/sw0goals.htm on April 21, 2015.

Ontario Ministry of Education. (2014). *The OFIP journey: 2003–04– 2013–14.* Accessed at https://ofip1415.files.wordpress.com/2014/10 /ofip-journey_2003_2013.pdf on March 21, 2015.

Organisation for Economic Co-operation and Development. (2005). *OECD average and OECD total.* Accessed at https://oecd.org/edu /school/programmeforinternationalstudentassessmentpisa/35002965 .pdf on May 29, 2017.

Organisation for Economic Co-operation and Development. (2014a). *Education at a glance 2014: Country note—United States.* Accessed at www.oecd.org/edu/United%20States-EAG2014-Country-Note .pdf on January 31, 2017.

Organisation for Economic Co-operation and Development. (2014b). *Education at a glance 2014: OECD indicators.* Accessed at www .oecd.org/edu/Education-at-a-Glance-2014.pdf on March 21, 2015.

Organisation for Economic Co-operation and Development. (2014c). *Measuring innovation in education: A new perspective.* Accessed at http://dx.doi.org/10.1787/9789264215696-en on January 31, 2017.

Pfeffer, J., & Sutton, R. I. (2006). *Hard facts, dangerous half-truths, and total nonsense: Profiting from evidence-based management.* Boston: Harvard Business School Press.

Plessy v. Ferguson, 163 U.S. 537 (1896).

Popham, W. J. (2011, February 22). Formative assessment—A process, not a test. *Education Week.* Accessed at www.edweek.org/ew/articles /2011/02/23/21popham.h30.html?qs=popham+inmeta:Authors% 3DW%252E%2520James%2520Popham on November 7, 2015.

Reeves, D. B. (2001). *Crusade in the classroom: How George W. Bush's education reforms will affect your children, our schools—A practical non-partisan guide to the changes and choices you can expect.* New York: Simon & Schuster.

Reeves, D. B. (2004). *Accountability in action: A blueprint for learning organizations* (2nd ed.). Englewood, CO: Advanced Learning Press.

Reeves, D. B. (2006). *The learning leader: How to focus school improvement for better results*. Alexandria, VA: Association for Supervision and Curriculum Development.

Reeves, D. B. (2009). *Leading change in your school: How to conquer myths, build commitment, and get results*. Alexandria, VA: Association for Supervision and Curriculum Development.

Reeves, D. B. (2011). *Finding your leadership focus: What matters most for student results*. New York: Teachers College Press.

Reeves, D. B. (2015). *Inspiring creativity and innovation in K–12*. Bloomington, IN: Solution Tree Press.

Roskos, K. A., Christie, J. F., & Richgels, D. J. (2003). *The essentials of early literacy instruction*. Accessed at www.naeyc.org/files/yc /file/200303/Essentials.pdf on July 10, 2016.

Rubin, J. (2015, April 24). A big legislative win on education. *The Washington Post*. Accessed at www.washingtonpost.com/blogs /right-turn/wp/2015/04/24/a-big-legislative-win-on-education /?utm_term=.e5017c306910 on May 31, 2017.

Saphier, J., Haley-Speca, M. A., & Gower, R. (2008). *The skillful teacher: Building your teaching skills* (6th ed.). Acton, MA: Research for Better Teaching.

Severns, M. (2015). *House passes No Child Left Behind rewrite*. Accessed at www.politico.com/story/2015/12/no-child-left-behind-congress -216371 on May 3, 2016.

Shavelson, R. J., Linn, R. L., Baker, E. L., Ladd, H. F., Darling-Hammond, L., Shepard, L. A., et al. (2010). *Problems with the use of student test scores to evaluate teachers* (Briefing Paper No. 278). Accessed at www.epi.org/publication/bp278 on October 17, 2016.

Shober, A. F. (2015, December 8). *ESEA reauthorization continues a long federal retreat from American classrooms* [Blog post]. Accessed at www.brookings.edu/blogs/brown-center-chalkboard/posts/2015 /12/08-esea-reauthorization-essa-shober on May 3, 2016.

Sloan, K. (2007). *Holding schools accountable: A handbook for educators and parents*. Westport, CT: Praeger.

Social Welfare History Project. (n.d.). *Elementary and Secondary Education Act of 1965*. Accessed at http://socialwelfare.library.vcu .edu/programs/education/elementary-and-secondary-education-act -of-1965/ on June 17, 2017.

Sparks, S. D. (2016, February 10). *OECD: U.S. efforts haven't helped low performers on global math, reading tests* [Blog post]. Accessed at http://blogs.edweek.org/edweek/inside-school-research/2016/02 /OECD_American_efforts_low_performers.html on January 31, 2017.

Stiggins, R. (2014). *Defensible teacher evaluation: Student growth through classroom assessment.* Thousand Oaks, CA: Corwin Press.

Thomas B. Fordham Institute. (2007). *Is No Child Left Behind's birthday worth celebrating?* Accessed at https://edexcellence.net/commentary /education-gadfly-weekly/2007/january-4/is-no-child-left-behinds -birthday-worth-celebrating-1.html on January 31, 2017.

Tucker, M. S. (2011). *Standing on the shoulders of giants: An American agenda for education reform.* Washington, DC: National Center on Education and the Economy. Accessed at http://ncee.org/wp -content/uploads/2011/05/Standing-on-the-Shoulders-of-Giants -An-American-Agenda-for-Education-Reform.pdf on January 31, 2017.

Tucker, M. S. (2014). *Fixing our national accountability system: Executive summary.* Washington, DC: National Center on Education and the Economy. Accessed at www.ncee.org/wp-content/uploads/2014/08 /FONAS-Executive-SummaryWeb1.pdf on March 21, 2015.

Ujifusa, A. (2016, September 12). *Assume you can do what you like under ESSA, Sen. Alexander tells Ky. lawmakers* [Blog post]. Accessed at http://blogs.edweek.org/edweek/campaign-k-12/2016/09/sen _alexander_essa_remarks_kentucky.html on January 31, 2017.

United States Census Bureau. (n.d.). *School districts.* Accessed at www .census.gov/did/www/schooldistricts on May 30, 2017.

U.S. Const., art. I, § 8.

U.S. Const. amend. X.

U.S. Const. amend. XIV.

U.S. Department of Education. (2003, August 23). *Fact sheet on the major provisions of the conference report to H.R. 1, the No Child Left Behind Act.* Accessed at www2.ed.gov/nclb/overview/intro/factsheet .html on March 20, 2015.

U.S. Department of Education. (2009). *Race to the Top program: Executive summary.* Accessed at www2.ed.gov/programs /racetothetop/executive-summary.pdf on March 20, 2015.

U.S. Department of Education. (2016, May 26). *Implementing the Every Student Succeeds Act to enhance equity and excellence* [Blog post]. Accessed at http://blog.ed.gov/2016/05/implementing-the-every-student-succeeds-act-to-enhance-equity-and-excellence on July 10, 2016.

U.S. Department of Education. (2017). *Budget history tables.* Accessed at www2.ed.gov/about/overview/budget/history/index.html on July 10, 2016.

Welner, K. G., & Mathis, W. J. (2015). *Reauthorization of the Elementary and Secondary Education Act: Time to move beyond test-focused policies.* Boulder: University of Colorado, National Education Policy Center. Accessed at http://nepc.colorado.edu/files/nepc-policymemo-esea.pdf on February 17, 2015.

Wong, A. (2015, December 9). The bloated rhetoric of No Child Left Behind's demise: What replacing the despised law actually means for America's schools. *The Atlantic.* Accessed at www.theatlantic.com/education/archive/2015/12/the-bloated-rhetoric-of-no-child-left-behinds-demise/419688 on May 31, 2017.

INDEX

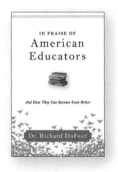

In Praise of American Educators
Richard DuFour
Explore the state of education today. The author establishes why contemporary American educators are the greatest generation in history and then presents specific steps policymakers and educators must take to transform American schools to meet student needs in the 21st century.
BKF702

Learning by Doing
Richard DuFour, Rebecca DuFour, Robert Eaker, Thomas W. Many, and Mike Mattos
The third edition of this comprehensive action guide includes new strategies, tools, and tips for transforming your school or district into a high-performing PLC.
BKF746

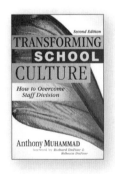

School Improvement for All
Sharon V. Kramer and Sarah Schuhl
Discover how to use the School Improvement for All framework to drive sustained school improvement and increase student achievement. Each chapter includes space for teacher teams to determine next action steps and a list of questions to help bring greater focus to improvement efforts.
BKF770

Transforming School Culture
Anthony Muhammad
Busy administrators will appreciate this quick read packed with immediate, accessible strategies. This second edition provides the framework for understanding dynamic relationships within a school culture and ensuring a positive environment that supports the changes necessary to improve learning for all students.
BKF793

a division of

Solution Tree | Press

Solution Tree

Visit SolutionTree.com or call 800.733.6786 to order.

GL⬤BAL **PD**

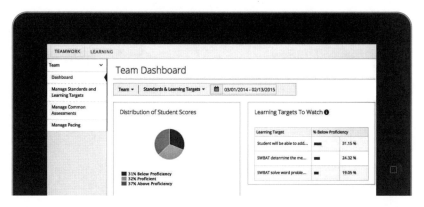

The **Power to Improve**
Is in Your Hands

Global PD gives educators focused and goals-oriented training from top experts. You can rely on this innovative online tool to improve instruction in every classroom.

- Get unlimited, on-demand access to guided video and book content from top Solution Tree authors.

- Improve practices with personalized virtual coaching from PLC-certified trainers.

- Customize learning based on skill level and time commitments.